**KILLED
IN
BRAZIL?**

HAMILCAR NOIR | TRUE CRIME LIBRARY #4

KILLED IN BRAZIL?

THE MYSTERIOUS DEATH OF ARTURO "THUNDER" GATTI

JIMMY TOBIN

HAMILCAR NOIR

HARD-HITTING TRUE CRIME

ISBN: 978-1949590-26-5

Publisher's Cataloging-in-Publication Data
Names: Tobin, Jimmy, author.
Title: Killed in Brazil? The mysterious death of Arturo "Thunder" Gatti / Jimmy Tobin.
Description: Boston, MA: Hamilcar Publications, An imprint of Hannibal Boxing Media, 2020.
Identifiers: LCCN: 2020933283 | ISBN: 9781949590265
Subjects: LCSH Gatti, Arturo, 1972–2009. | Boxing—History—21st century. | Boxers (Sports)—Biography. | BISAC SPORTS & RECREATION / Boxing | BIOGRAPHY & AUTOBIOGRAPHY / Sports | TRUE CRIME / Murder / General
Classification: LCC GV1132.G36 T63 2020 | DDC 796.830922–dc23

Hamilcar Publications
An imprint of Hannibal Boxing Media
Ten Post Office Square, 8th Floor South
Boston, MA 02109
www.hamilcarpubs.com

Printed in the United Kingdom

On the cover: Arturo Gatti enters the ring for his welterweight fight against Alfonso Gomez on July 14, 2007, at Boardwalk Hall in Atlantic City. (Al Bello/Getty Images)

Frontispiece: Arturo Gatti celebrates knocking out Jesse James Leija to defend the WBC super-lightweight world title at Boardwalk Hall on January 29, 2005, in Atlantic City. (Al Bello/Getty Images)

For Rachel and Oliver. And for Margaret.

Fracture

*"Terrible things happen all the time.
This is the terrible thing."*
—Martin Amis, *The Killings in Atlanta*

When Amanda Gatti went to bed the night of July 10, 2009, she thought her marriage was over. "Don't go to bed angry," that piece of marital wisdom, like so much of its kind easier to prescribe than follow, seemed futile in a moment of such fracture. The night's volcanic and far-too-public fight had exhausted her. She crawled into bed and waited for sleep to deliver her from the trials of the night, to prepare her for the morning and the trials it must bring.

A few hours before sunrise, Amanda descended the stairs of her suite in Hotel Dorisol, Porto de Galinha, a seaside resort in Pernambuco, Brazil, where she was on a second honeymoon of sorts with her husband, iconic boxer Arturo Gatti, and their ten-month-old son, Arturo Junior. The baby needed his bottle. Out of the corner of her eye, she could see her husband. He looked as he might reasonably be expected to considering his behavior only hours earlier: naked but for his underwear, a crumpled heap. Knocked out.

She'd seen it before, suffered it before, too. Gatti was, in Amanda's words, "a completely different man when he was drinking." And he'd been drinking. The crowd outside the pizzeria that served as the setting for their latest fight could attest to that. So could her body, bruised and bloodied as it was. Drunk, angry with her for refusing to join him at a local bar, Gatti had shoved her to the ground.

"He wouldn't let me take my son," she would later admit. So, hurt and exhausted, she left Gatti with their son, who was asleep in his stroller.

When she came back to their room sometime later, Amanda found Gatti sitting, his arms around a crying Junior, his blood spattered on the baby's bib. Amanda didn't yet know it, but a crowd had witnessed Gatti assault her. It responded with street justice. After she left the bar to return to the suite a mob twenty-deep attacked the boxer. Gatti fought back in a rage but bore the marks of a man hit by fists, rocks, even a bicycle.

"I guess it's over, huh?" he asked. Resorting to a question can be easier than stating the answer—especially an answer you don't want to hear, don't want to speak. A question retains some hope. A question can be a dare.

"It's over," she told him before going up to bed.

So Amanda said nothing to her husband as she came down the stairs in the early morning, perhaps because with him in that contorted repose, in his peace, she found a little of her own. Perhaps because there was nothing to say, nothing left to fight for—and no fight left. Not enough anyway. Junior needed his bottle, too, and whatever closure she might reach with her husband, at that groggy hour it came second to the needs of their son.

Back to bed then, bottle in hand. Imagine her stealing another glance as she crept up the stairs. Did she narrow her eyes at the cause of so much of her pain or shake her head in disgust? Did she breathe a heavy sigh for him, for their family, and maybe with it feel her resolve soften just a bit? It is a terrible thing to break up a family, after all.

What the morning brought was worse.

Around nine in the morning, Amanda made her way back downstairs, still upset, still ready to say goodbye. This time she went to him, shook him. He was cold. Face-down. A halo of blood fanned out around his head. A knife lay nearby. The anger that had fortified her nerve, that had fixed her jaw as she came down to confront the aftermath of the night, disappeared.

"Arturo, I forgive you! Please wake up! Please wake up, Arturo!"

Then came the screams.

"My husband's dead! My husband's dead! Please, someone, help me!"

▼ ▼ ▼

Alone in that hotel room with her baby—the body of her dead husband, so powerfully inanimate, anchoring her to a nightmare she wished only to escape—Amanda needed help, alright. But dead bodies demand an explanation, and once she was safely removed from the scene, Amanda was expected to explain as best—as convincingly—as she could what happened. More specifically, she was expected to explain her role in it. The first explanation left the twenty-three-year-old suddenly single mother in desperate need of help again.

▼ ▼ ▼

Amanda Rodrigues was arrested in Recife, Brazil, on July 12, 2009, the primary suspect in her husband's murder. If she had felt alone the morning before, it was nothing like the sense of isolation she felt now, separated from her baby, in the custody of Brazilian police. Yes, dead bodies demand an explanation, and at that stage of the investigation the most likely explanation for Gatti's death was that he'd been murdered by his wife. There were strangulation marks on Gatti's neck, marks that seemed to have been caused by the blood-stained purse strap found at the scene. The assumption among Brazilian law enforcement was that Amanda had strangled a drunken Gatti while he slept, a state that would've allowed her to overpower a man who not only outweighed her by some seventy pounds but who knocked people cold for a living.

Moreover, she acted alone. This much was confirmed by Mosies Teixeira, the lead investigator in the case. Teixeira told the Associated Press that it was "technically impossible for a third person to have been in the flat." There were no signs of forced entry and the electronic locks on the door confirmed that no one other than Amanda and Gatti had entered the unit. "The investigation isn't finished," said Teixeira, "but we continue to think she did this alone." Teixeira's suggestion that the investigation had not yet ruled anything out misrepresented the matter somewhat. What had been ruled out thus far was the possibility that Amanda acted with an accomplice. And implicit in that belief was the assumption she had acted.

Amanda was less certain about what happened. In her version of the story, she had been sleeping, ignorant of the ending being engineered downstairs. She suggested Gatti might have killed himself, or that someone might have somehow entered the apartment and murdered him. She was innocent, however, on this she could accept no doubt.

Teixeira dismissed both explanations. Brazilian law dictates that although police accuse a person of a crime, the prosecutor is responsible for formally filing a charge. Police had until July 22 to share their findings with the prosecutor, and it boded poorly for Amanda that Teixeira, already analyzing the case as a murder, hoped to have the investigation completed before the deadline. Ten years later, Main Events CEO Kathy Duva would come back to this point in explaining her sense of what happened that night. "That they arrested her immediately tells me they had good reason to think that she did it."

Seemingly unfazed by Teixeira's expectations, Amanda welcomed a speedy resolution. In a letter from prison, she wrote: "I am innocent, and I know that this will be proven in a few days."

▼▼▼

A few days? Not given the evidence. The early defenses offered on Amanda's behalf were unlikely to dissuade Teixeira. Amanda offered one herself, sharing a letter she wrote from jail with the Associated Press on July 15. In it, she stressed the strength of her bond with her husband. "The people most important to my life," she wrote, "who know us, know the size of our love." Speaking to her suffering, she continued: "What hurts me is knowing the suffering of my family and friends. What hurts me is to know that my husband will not be in my house waiting for my return."

Confronted with the possibility of Amanda somehow being a murderer, with the despair of having to reevaluate their image of her as a result, Amanda's family urged the world to understand her as they did. In an interview with TV Jornal, a Recife news station, Amanda's sister, Flavia, expressed her family's support: "Amanda told us that she didn't kill Arturo, and we believe her," she said, adding, "My sister, like us, is very religious and would be incapable of killing anyone."

Leaving aside that very religious people often commit murder, the use of "like us" here is telling. It is an attempt to confine Amanda to a context where murder is an aberration, unthinkable. In the context of the family, Amanda couldn't be a murderer. It was membership in a group, in their group, that made Amanda's guilt impossible for her family. The Gatti family would use a similar logic in their steadfast refusal to believe one of their own could take his own life.

Even Flavia, who gave no ground in defending her sister's innocence, struggled to understand Gatti's suicide. Nor could she understand what might precipitate the kind of fight between the two that would result in tragedy. "Sure they had fights," said Flavia, "but he was crazy about her." Amanda and Arturo didn't just have fights, though. To suggest as much was either naive or dishonest. The dysfunction in their marriage would come to light. And when it did, it would take more than character witnesses to see Amanda exonerated.

For now, though, the puzzling physics of the crime scene were in Amanda's favor. Speaking to Brazilian newspaper *Folha de S.Paulo*, Flavia argued that Amanda could not have strangled her husband, who physically dwarfed her. It was a line of argument echoed by Celio Avelino, Amanda's attorney: "She is fragile, young and skinny—how could she kill a boxing champion?" he asked. A fair question, though one that excluded some pertinent details. What about Gatti's inebriation, the injuries he suffered at the hands of that angry mob? Avelino wasn't finished though. Even had Amanda succeeded in subduing and strangling Gatti in his drunken state, she still had to suspend him from the stairs, and from a height of seven feet. That too seemed a physical impossibility. Avelino believed these feats eliminated Amanda as a murder suspect. "When she awoke," he said, "she presumed he had committed suicide. But she had nothing to do with it." This statement, too, is a little curious, if only because it introduced another possibility. The possibility that Gatti committed suicide, and that Amanda had played a role in his doing so.

▼▼▼

That Amanda had nothing to do with her husband's death is something the Brazilian police eventually accepted. On July 30, they ruled Gatti's death a suicide. Police official Paulo Alberes told the Brazilian newspaper *Diário de Pernambuco* that Gatti used Amanda's purse strap to hang himself from the hotel-room staircase. "The case has been resolved," said police spokeswoman Milena Saraiva. "While the evidence at the scene first led us to think Gatti was murdered, the autopsy results and a detailed crime-scene analysis simply pointed to a different outcome."

After nearly three weeks in jail, Amanda was released when judge Ildete Verissimo de Lima ruled that there were no grounds for retaining a suspect in an investigation that excluded the possibility of murder.

The final moments of Gatti's life then, in the eyes of Brazilian police, were entirely his own.

Grimly fashioning a noose, adjusting it for size, positioning a stool, calculating the stability of his makeshift gallows—alone in this despairing ritual, one imagines, despite the world around him, despite the reason for living asleep upstairs. He had to climb the stool too. His body betraying him from the "seven cans of beer, along with two bottles of wine" he'd consumed at dinner, betraying him from the head injury he'd suffered when that mob attacked him for throwing Amanda to the ground. Did he stand resolutely atop that stool, his faulty balance countered by the firmness of his resolve? Did he think of the wife he would leave permanently, the son who may never grasp why he was separated from the man whose name he shared, that unforgettable man he could never fully remember? Did Gatti think he was giving up? Did he think he had a choice?

These are questions an autopsy can't answer. And Gatti, leaving no suicide note, left them unanswerable, lost forever at the thud of a toppled stool.

▼ ▼ ▼

So many questions left to be answered by the people who cared most for him. And these people couldn't agree on an answer. Amanda had her own explanation for Gatti's suicide. "I believe that when we got home and he saw he hurt me, he thought I would leave him, that I would tell him to just let me go, that I would separate from him," she told the Associated Press after walking out of jail. "He did that in a moment of weakness. He was drunk, maybe he didn't know what he was doing, maybe he thought I would leave him the next day."

A charitable treatment of this explanation might read as follows: a new widow, one who discovered her husband's dead body, who spent nearly three weeks in jail while being investigated for murder, who answered countless questions about her knowledge of the events that widowed and jailed her, provided the only explanation she could imagine.

As far as explanations go, it is a poor one, maybe understandably so, but a poor one nonetheless. Because while Amanda might well have been about to leave Gatti in the morning, it is hard to imagine that Gatti, even in his despair, would consider a failed marriage reason enough to make his two children—Junior as well as a daughter from a previous relationship—fatherless. Yes, it appeared like he and Amanda were trying to salvage

7

a tumultuous marriage with their second honeymoon. And yes, Gatti's friends and family pleaded with him to escape a toxic relationship. But he told them he'd submit to a spin on the marital Catherine Wheel to preserve his relationship with Junior.

Accepting—as many did not—that Gatti and Amanda were trying to find happiness together does little to make Amanda's explanation more satisfying. If their union was so strong, so important that ending it would show the world what Gatti was ultimately capable of, why couldn't Amanda provide greater insight into what drove him to suicide? Granted, she may not have known him any better than anyone else. Their relationship was only a few years old. It can take much longer than that to learn who a person is, especially if they're afraid to lose you. Still, Amanda's explanation for Gatti's death hinged on the importance of her in his life and his drunkenness. And that may have been all she could honestly offer. She didn't have to offer more given the conclusions of the police investigation (her explanation was mostly immaterial where that was concerned). But it did little to dampen suspicions.

▼ ▼ ▼

Just how strong was the bond between the two, anyway? In a phone interview she gave shortly after Gatti died, his mother Ida said that the couple was always fighting, that Amanda was "yelling all the time," telling Gatti "I'm going to kill you!" And there was hostility in more than their speech. In April of that year, Gatti violated a restraining order filed against him. Who filed the restraining order wasn't clear in the record but Ida confirmed it was Amanda. She had called 911 claiming that Gatti hit her. He was charged with assault and released on bail. Gatti was ordered to stay two hundred yards away from Amanda and to abstain from alcohol. Not that he did; not that Amanda wanted him to.

Then there is Duva's story about the night she learned Gatti died. It was July 11. Duva was standing in her kitchen when her phone rang.

Rick Reeno of boxingscene.com was on the other end. "Did you hear the news?"

"I thought it was a hoax," remembers Duva. It wasn't, and so with Gatti's manager, Pat Lynch, in Italy, she traveled to the Prudential Center in Newark, where Tomasz Adamek was fighting Bobby Gunn. Gatti's friends were at the fight, and Duva made it her duty to break the awful news. She remembers walking through the arena, telling Gatti's friends as she saw them. One of his friends responded in a way Duva has never forgotten:

"She finally killed him."

"The people that were closest to him," says Duva, remembering all those difficult exchanges, "this was their reaction."

This was the same reaction Gatti's younger brother Fabricio had to the news. "The first thing that popped into my mind? She killed him." At a time when the details were unclear, when there was little more to process than loss and shock, mariticide was the only explanation for those who knew Gatti best.

Further domestic dysfunction was revealed in 2011 when the Gatti family tried to annul the final version of Gatti's will (a will that left everything to Amanda). In Quebec's Superior Court, Gatti's friend, Antonio Rizzo, testified to the marriage's stormy nature. Rizzo said it was a union marked by continuous fights, that Gatti had become increasingly worried that Amanda might take Junior from him, and feared what she was capable of while in Brazil. Recounting a conversation he had with Gatti about this fear, Rizzo remembers his friend saying, "She wants me to sign a Brazilian passport for him. But if she takes my son I'll never see him again." These fears weren't the product of paranoia either. Duva remembers Lynch sharing a story of a neighbor who lost custody of his child when his wife left for Brazil with their baby. It was Duva's understanding that, second honeymoon or not, Gatti was going to Brazil to come home with Junior, and that on his return he planned to change his will once more.

Throughout his testimony, Rizzo apologized to the court for replicating the language Amanda used in her fights with Gatti. He told the court about a night at the couple's penthouse on Jarry Street in Saint-Leonard, Quebec. Amanda, screaming, hit Gatti over the head with a broom, smashed crystal all around him, and demanding he clean up the mess. "You're a loser," Amanda told him, "the only thing you're good at is bleeding, your mother's a whore, your sisters are prostitutes." Rodrigues's lawyer objected to the story on the grounds of it being hearsay and therefore inadmissible. But it is hard to unhear such things.

Rizzo wasn't the only person in Gatti's life who had seen that side of Amanda. Gatti's childhood friend, Chris Santos, offered testimony that supported Rizzo's depiction of the Gatti marriage. He, too, said Amanda was "foul-mouthed and bad-tempered" and had once given Gatti a black eye. Amanda herself testified to keying her husband's truck after an argument. The incident produced $4,000 in damages. In the police report Gatti filed that night, Amanda was listed as his ex-wife. Details like these Amanda tried to explain away as idiosyncrasies of her marriage, incidents that, for the uninitiated, appeared worse than they were.

At times, money was at the root of these eruptions. Despite a notary giving the court a copy of Gatti's last will and testament, Rizzo said Gatti complained in the months before his death of the pressure from Amanda to leave his estate to her. "I told him: 'It's fine. You have two kids, your relationship is upside-down,'" testified Rizzo, "'You leave half to your daughter and half to your son.'" Gatti's response? "'You don't understand. Amanda wants me to leave everything to her. I will never do that.'"

Then there was the voicemail Gatti left Rizzo, a voicemail Rizzo saved for years after. At the time he left it, Gatti was in Amsterdam, on the European leg of his trip with Amanda and Junior. That trip had started in Paris, where Gatti surprised Amanda with a romantic trip up the Eiffel Tower. While taking in the view, Gatti had champagne brought over. There was a diamond ring in Amanda's flute, a gift from her husband.

Amanda said it was here that Gatti apologized for his behavior, that he swore he would mend his ways for his family.

There is none of that optimism in the voicemail.

"Yo Tony, you were fuckin' right," said Gatti in the voicemail. "It's a fuckin' nightmare. I'll talk to you later, alright? I'm gonna be back sooner than I expected. Ciao." This sounded nothing like a man recommitting to his marriage. It sounded very much, however, like the words of a man who spent some of his marriage living in his mom's basement instead of going home to his wife. "A world champion. Living in a basement," remembers Rizzo. "Incredible."

▼▼▼

It hadn't always been that way. Duva recalls Gatti excitedly introducing Amanda and her family to his inner circle at a fight. He said she was a student, that they met walking their dogs. "She didn't look like a student," remembers Duva, but Gatti wouldn't discuss the matter any further. The real story, many people hold, is that Amanda met Gatti at Squeeze Lounge, a New Jersey gentlemen's club where she worked as an exotic dancer. Former employees of the establishment have corroborated that story. Amanda vehemently denies it. There is no record of her being an employee of Squeeze Lounge, and she has taken legal action against news organizations that claimed she was. But a photo of her in the club wearing a bikini has fueled suspicions regardless.

For Duva, there was something a bit peculiar about the Rodrigues family too. She remembers being struck by how happy they were, exhibiting a strange amount of joy at the new relationship. Gatti was smitten, enamored with a girl he was convinced liked him for who he was—not for his fame, not for his money, but for his charming and fun self. Was Gatti right? Had he found in Amanda—who was slack-jawed when she found out he earned his living in the cruelest sport—someone drawn to the man he was away from the spotlight, the crowds, the fast life? Or was

11

Gatti succumbing to a willful naivete? It isn't hard to understand why he might want someone who desired a quieter, less destructive version of himself. Mario Costa, who owns the Ringside Lounge, a bar next door to the gym a nineteen-year-old Gatti joined when he moved to Jersey City, said the fighter "lived in go-go bars." Costa saw Gatti's life as one desperately lacking structure.

If it was structure, peace, even a sort of amorous innocence Gatti was looking for, however, there is little evidence that he found it with Amanda. "He had terrible taste in women," recalls Duva. "And the one woman who really cared about him [Erika Rivera, his ex-fiancée and mother of his first child, Sofia], she really couldn't take it." There is a nod here to Gatti's wild side, of its prohibitive force, and perhaps in that an explanation for his poor taste in women. It may be difficult to find a girl to settle down with when you never settle down yourself. Still, women troubles aside, Gatti "was really good at picking his friends," said Duva, a tinge of regret softening her voice, "I just wish he would have taken his friends' advice."

▼▼▼

In a sad irony, the girl who Gatti believed loved him for him, ended up embroiled in a bitter dispute over his money. His family sued to have the will that left Amanda the beneficiary of his estate declared invalid.

The fight over Gatti's will hangs over and lays beneath the entire ordeal of his death. Like so many before, it was a fight Gatti was supposed to have ended with his own hand. That this struggle persisted after his death does him a disservice. He had left his affairs in order or at least assumed he had. This can be a courtesy the dying leave the living, a gesture of love and consideration for those left behind. But in another sense, Gatti's will wasn't a courtesy to the living, it was an act of extortion— extortion he intended to overcome once he returned to the United States. In its devotion to Amanda, Gatti's will was evidence of her innocence.

But that devotion is also suspicious. Rewritten so close to his mysterious death, Gatti's will can also be interpreted as a placating gesture performed to appease the mother of his son, a woman whose ability to tear him from his son left Gatti fearful. More, it is a motive for murder. Submitting, even temporarily, to the pressures of his wife, Gatti left everything to her before departing for a foreign country where he died violently while she slept only feet away. The timing was too convenient: if Amanda was going to kill her husband, it made sense to secure her fortune first. The will can't be all of these things at once, either Gatti killed himself or he was murdered. But if nothing else, Gatti's will reveals the touch of madness in his marriage.

Montreal notary Bruce Moidel was responsible for drafting the final version of Gatti's will. He testified in the civil trial. Moidel remembers his meeting with the couple as "a normal, typical meeting for a young couple about to fly off and leave a baby behind with family" (Arturo Jr. did not accompany the Gattis on the first leg of their vacation). But that impression flipped quickly. As the trio worked their way through the will's details, Amanda began to air mistrust of her husband. She seemed convinced that Gatti would one day be unfaithful. Where such jealousy might figure in drafting a will is unclear, but it proved to have financial consequences. Straining to convince his wife of his devotion, Gatti told Amanda he'd give her a million dollars in the event he was unfaithful. And he wasn't just talking. Moidel eventually drafted an agreement accompanying the will stating that if Gatti ever cheated on Amanda he would have to give her the money. Moidel, who became a notary in 1958, admitted he'd never encountered a measure like that, and that it was entirely the work of the couple.

Was Gatti unfaithful? Did Amanda have reasons for doubting him? The answers to those questions have yet to breach the silent respect for the dead. Gatti's gesture, however, in its overcompensation, is difficult to interpret as anything but an indictment of his marriage.

▼ ▼ ▼

It looked to many like the Gattis had exhausted their life together. Yet even if that were true, might Gatti not have retained some perspective on what a future without Amanda could promise? After all, he "loved his children, traveling, enjoying his retirement," said Lynch, "[h]e was happy, upbeat, and enjoyed life. He had too much to lose." Interestingly, for Lynch, Amanda did not figure in the list of things that Gatti found joy in. That may have been a coincidence, but maybe not. This omission suggests that Amanda's absence from Gatti's life would make it no less worth living.

There is evidence Gatti himself was unconvinced of the emptiness of a world without Amanda. Days after their 2007 wedding, Gatti visited a New Jersey lawyer with Amanda to tear up a copy of the couple's pre-nuptial agreement. That agreement left Amanda with nothing in the case of divorce, not even alimony. According to The Canadian Press, Amanda testified that Gatti destroyed a copy of the agreement as an unsolic-ited gesture of his love for her. Does this testimony really contrast with the one Rizzo provided, which depicted Gatti as a man fearful of not appearing devoted?

This ceremonial shredding may have been a gesture of love, but Gatti made sure the prenuptial agreement remained valid. By 2009, when the couple's marriage was experiencing periods of increasing turmoil, Gatti asked his lawyer in New Jersey to send a copy of the agreement to his divorce attorney in Montreal. Amanda too had been in contact with a divorce attorney by this time. Even the momentary nihilism that might have precipitated Gatti's suicide, then, seems out of place. Gatti had loved, lost, and recovered; he was capable of planning responsibly. There is futurity in these legal proceedings that makes Gatti's suicide puzzling. A man planning for his future does so because he intends to have one.

We accept that love can kill. The world has its share of suf-fering Werthers who, unable to obtain their sole desire, embrace a liberating nothingness. But the love between Amanda and Gatti wasn't unrequited—they were on a second honeymoon, with their baby no less. Loss too can precipitate suicide. It's called "the widowhood effect," a term used to capture what is, according to the *British Medical Journal*, a strong association between spousal bereavement and death.

To see Amanda walk through the iron doors of a Brazilian jail, smiling and waving in the bursts of flashbulbs like a coy paparazzi obsession, was to see a woman who looked anything but bereaved. Perhaps this isn't fair, reading into the body language of a woman moments into her freedom a perhaps criminal absence of sadness. And yet it is an image that stuck in the craw of Gatti's friends and family. So maybe it isn't right to say that analyzing Amanda's behavior as she crossed the threshold into freedom is unfair. It might be unfair if she were innocent. But there were a lot of people who doubted she was.

By the letter of the law, of course, Amanda was indeed innocent. Still, Gatti's family and friends remained unconvinced by the police investigation's results. What they saw in Amanda's smile was the satisfaction of a woman who'd gotten away with murder. And they were going to wipe that smile from her face.

▼▼▼

The first step for the Gatti family was requesting a second autopsy. The initial autopsy indicated that Gatti "may have committed suicide." It failed to rule out the possibility that he didn't. Canada's Minister of Foreign Affairs, Lawrence Cannon, supported the family's request for a second autopsy, formally asking Brazilian authorities for further information about the case. According to forensic pathologist Satish Chundru, a second autopsy is most commonly requested by the family of the deceased to get information or answers to questions the first autopsy couldn't satisfy. Not only were the Gattis unsatisfied by the findings of the first autopsy—they were suspicious of it. Gatti's older brother

Joe suspected the Brazilian authorities of trying to exonerate Amanda. "Everything points to her," said Joe, as the suicide speculation first picked up, "No doubt they're trying to get her off." Lynch echoed Joe's sentiment, saying, "Everyone who knew him would know that's [suicide] far from the truth."

On July 30, Gatti was classified a suicide in the eyes of the law. The next day he was exhumed to test the validity of that classification. Speaking on the Gatti family's decision to challenge the suicide verdict, Avelino seemed unthreatened: "Gatti's family was first told by police that Amanda had killed him, and now they are saying he committed suicide. Of course, family and friends have doubts and are demanding another autopsy, as they should." But he reiterated his confidence in Amanda's innocence: "I am absolutely sure that the second autopsy will reconfirm that he committed suicide."

The second autopsy was performed by coroners from the Gatti family's native Quebec. Michael Baden, the former chief pathologist for the New York State Police and host of the television show *Autopsy,* also participated at the family's request. He revealed the team's findings in an interview with the Associated Press.

"There were some surprises," said Baden. The first surprise was that the initial autopsy was a partial autopsy, not a full autopsy. That difference is significant. The problem with a partial autopsy is that it may examine areas of the body that do not furnish the cause of death, or in focusing on specific areas of the body, it may fail to notice evidence not found in those specific areas. This is why, according to the Autopsy Center of Chicago, a partial autopsy "cannot definitively determine the cause of death." Only a complete autopsy can do so. It is for this reason that partial autopsies, according to Baden, are unusual in suspected homicides. Gatti's death had initially been treated like a homicide, but he hadn't been given the proper autopsy for such a case. Had he been given one, Brazilian investigators would have found what Baden did. Among Baden's discoveries were injuries that went undetected in the first autopsy. Baden admitted that any conclusions about Gatti's death would require both the toxicology report and "results from the Brazilian police as to the scene of death and circumstances in Brazil."

Here was a glimmer of hope for the Gatti family: Baden was essentially saying that the findings of the second autopsy, at least as of August 1, 2009, did not rule out the possibility of homicide. What's more, there was now reason to criticize the quality of the investigation and the conclusions drawn from it.

While Gatti's family waited for his body to tell its story, Amanda decided it was time to tell hers.

▼▼▼

"I didn't even have the chance to go to my husband's funeral." On August 13, 2009, *Le Journal de Montréal* published a letter Amanda wrote about her ordeal, and there is no more agonizing line in it than this. Interestingly, she doesn't address her husband's death so much as the fallout from it. It is thoughtful and exhaustive, reading like the product of revision and very likely legal counsel. For all that, it is the line about Gatti's funeral that stays with you. It seems unlikely, however, given the tone of the letter, that this sentence is particularly calculated, which only serves to better drive its point home. That point is that so long as Gatti died by his own hand, Amanda herself was a victim. She was a victim of the legal system that held her captive for nearly three weeks, a victim of the Gatti family's unjustified scorn and suspicion, even a victim of Gatti, who left her as the most likely explanation for the unthinkable.

"I didn't even have the chance to go to my husband's funeral."

The rest of the letter? It is anything but the work of a victim.

With her letter Amanda did more than open up about what she'd suffered in the previous weeks, more than express her love for her husband

and for the family that helped her through his suicide. In that letter, Amanda made clear the animosity that existed between her and her late husband's family.

"The worst accusations came from Gatti's family. Family with whom I've never had any intimacy. Not because I didn't want to or didn't like them," but because, she writes "my own husband was never 'that' close with his own family." How to make sense of this opening jab, one directed at the very people still pursuing what they believed to be justice for Gatti? Surely bearing the financial and emotional burden of continuing to investigate his death is proof that the Gattis were closer than Amanda said? If she misrepresented the Gatti family intentionally, why she might have done so becomes clear in the subsequent paragraph.

"When I heard that they want the custody of my child [sic], I was in shock." It was the Gatti's interest in Junior that had Amanda on the attack. "Only Arturo's mom and stepfather showed care and love for my baby. They never bothered to come to my house. I had my son far away from my family. Arturo was the only person who helped me in all aspects with my son. I have never received any visit or help from any member of his family. Arturo's family are not in any condition to take care of my son, neither psychologically nor financially." If the family truly believed Amanda killed Gatti, they were right to want to separate the baby from a murderer. But were there other motivations at work too? Was Junior serving as leverage in the looming battle for Gatti's estate? Amanda certainly believed so. "The only reason they would want the custody of my son would be for financial reasons," she writes.

Turning to her husband's troubled time in retirement, she admits that Gatti struggled with drugs and alcohol, but that she herself had checked him into rehab. "During this time I didn't hear from his family. I just heard from his sister when she picked him up three days before he was supposed to finish." Her story is corroborated by Les Perreaux in a 2011 article for *The Globe and Mail*. Perreaux writes that Amanda convinced Gatti to go to rehab in Florida in December 2007 and that Anna-Maria

Gatti indeed picked him up before his treatment was complete. "Big sister maintains to this day he didn't need it," wrote Perreaux.

Fabricio is treated with especially rough hands. According to Amanda, Fabricio wanted to be supported financially by his brother and that, as Gatti's wife, this was something she couldn't accept. Fabricio traveled to Brazil to arrange for his brother's body to be transported back to Montreal. In the letter, Amanda says he made no real effort to contact her during this time. She found the lack of contact curious since Fabricio had access to her email address and both her mother's and sister's phone numbers. She heard from Fabricio only once while he was in Brazil. The only thing he asked? "Where is Gatti's watch?"

"What I find very strange," writes Amanda, "is that if it was my sister, I would want to know every little detail about the incident. In his police report, the only thing he mentioned was about my financial life. Everything that came from his family so far was about financial issues."

For Amanda, Gatti's family saw her less as a murderer and more as an obstruction to acquiring Gatti's estate. "What really bothers Arturo's family is not the fact that he is not here anymore or the reason why he is not here. It's the simple fact that they are not included in the will. I know that even after the private autopsy, when it is proven for the second time that I did not do any harm to my husband, they will still be against me, claiming and fighting in the expectation of receiving anything regarding Arturo's estate."

Amanda wasn't wrong predicting the ugliness of the estate battle. And it wasn't only the family she was in conflict with. Perreaux spoke to Erika Rivera, mother to Gatti's first child, as well. At that time, Gatti's family was still fighting Amanda's claim to her husband's estate. There had been some progress made, however, and the dispute seemed headed for settlement. Erika, in the words of Perreaux, "brought discussions to a halt. She also launched her own wrongful death lawsuit against Ms. Rodrigues in New Jersey, putting a freeze on the money and ensuring nothing will be settled for years."

In the article, Erika is blunt and unforgiving in her treatment of Amanda, telling Perreaux, "I thought she'd be in jail by now. And if she won't go to jail, we'll take away the money. The only way this gets settled is with her not getting one red cent." Why might she draw this battle line so sharply? For the same reason Amanda did: her child's future. Erika hadn't become embroiled in the legalities of Gatti's estate until she "started getting legal documents in the mail that appeared to threaten her daughter's trust accounts set up by Mr. Gatti." Once that happened, she too declared war.

Yet Amanda had addressed the financial care of Gatti's daughter in her letter. "Arturo would never let anything miss for his daughter. The will explains with details what she gets. Sofia Bella Gatti owns two accounts— one for her college fund, and another as her trust account." This too is corroborated by Perreaux, who provided financial details of Sofia's inheritance. Gatti set up a $1.1 million trust, a trust approved by Amanda, that paid Erika $4,640 a month in child support. He also set aside $350,000 for Sofia in the second trust account. While financially present in his daughter's life, Gatti had decided to play a reduced role in her upbringing, something Amanda attributes to "problems that he had with his daughter's mother." As for problems Amanda may have had with Erika, Amanda said she "never asked Gatti or his family members (who also had no contact with his daughter) to stop seeing his daughter, because before anything I am still a mother."

Again Amanda found an opportunity to discredit the Gatti family. Indeed her letter seems motivated by this goal above all else. The question some might ask is, why? Why slander her in-laws? There are a couple of reasons that come to mind quickly. Decorum no longer demanded that she bite her tongue; she told her in-laws exactly how she felt about them and their lack of support for her in those critical days. On the other hand, she may have been controlling the narrative in the looming battle for her husband's estate. It is easy to imagine Amanda as the abandoned widow, and to empathize with her effort to reconstruct her life. But that effort didn't exist in a vacuum. Amanda's grief and frustration existed not only in her private moments or in the company of loved ones. Amanda was before the court of public opinion, a skeptical court still coming to terms with the mysterious loss of a beloved figure. To survive, Amanda needed to be more than a widow. She needed to be more than just innocent. And so in her letter Amanda was more than both. She was an exonerated victim who spat at the feet of her accusers as she walked out of the courtroom.

As the work of a murderer the letter works too. It diverts attention away from suspicions about Amanda's guilt, depicts her as a woman unfairly attacked by a conniving and unloving clan, and positions her favorably for the final phase in a scheme to take her husband's millions. But there is nothing particularly egregious about the Gatti's reaction to Arturo's death. Settling the affairs of a loved one can be a protracted and tedious process. It demands decisiveness, action, especially in Gatti's case, where there were children involved, millions on the line, and an inevitable court battle brewing. If the Gatti's were trying to save Arturo's estate from the woman who killed him for it there was no reason to be tender or patient. And if Amanda was the person they believed her to be, if she was the person so many of Gatti's friends believed her to be, the Gatti's were treating her like the threat she represented.

▼ ▼ ▼

Amanda expected the second autopsy to not only reveal her innocence but to reiterate it. But did it? Quebec coroner Jean Brochu said the second autopsy failed to produce any hard evidence that Gatti was killed. He concluded that the boxer died a violent death, the probable cause being "asphyxiation by neck constriction." Most important, Brochu found no indication of foul play. "Much of the debate surrounding the circumstances of the death revolved around the question of whether a third party was involved in Gatti's death," wrote Brochu. "The conclusion of the Montreal pathologists to the effect that there is no clear evidence of foul play in Mr. Gatti's death means I cannot dismiss the formal conclusions reached by the authorities of the country where it occurred."

Brochu left room for doubt, however, in his assessment of the initial police work. "The methods used by Brazilian investigators in examining the scene of Arturo Gatti's death," wrote Brochu, "can raise doubts, and so (I believe) that the circumstances of death cannot be determined with certainty." According to Brochu, the Brazilian investigation fell short of Canadian policing standards and mishandled evidence at the crime scene.

Mishandled evidence wasn't the only reason to be skeptical of the suicide conclusion. Martin Laliberte, the pathologist consulted for the second autopsy, found Carisoprodol in Gatti's system. Carisoprodol is a muscle-relaxant that, while in wide use elsewhere, was not available in Canada at the time. Sedating and habit-forming, and with withdrawal symptoms—including "anxiety, confusion, and psychosis"—that can last days, Carisoprodol is no longer readily available. It has been replaced by drugs with less dramatic side effects. But this drug, one that figured frequently in cases of death and suicide, was in Gatti's system. And for Laliberte, that presence raised questions about Gatti's mental state when he died.

Those questions had particular significance when paired with some of Brochu's more mysterious observations. To test their theory that Gatti hanged himself from the banister using a strap from Amanda's purse, Brazilian authorities hung a thirty-five-kilogram weight from the strap. It snapped in five seconds. How, then, did Gatti's seventy-kilogram body suspend from the strap long enough to cause his death? For Brochu, there was "no rational or satisfactory explanation to how this happened."

Lynch thought he had a rational and satisfactory explanation, however. "He was obviously drugged and then hung," he reasoned. "No one is going to convince me that Gatti committed suicide and took his own life in Brazil. And as more information comes out it will be concluded that it was a murder."

There was enough mystery in the second autopsy to doubt Gatti committed suicide. His inner circle had doubted it the entire time. They weren't alone. Boxing aficionados everywhere met the suicide explanation with skepticism. To understand why requires more than an understanding of forensics—the forensics, after all, didn't disprove the suicide explanation. It didn't take intimate knowledge of who Gatti was either. How many people who packed the Boardwalk or crowded around a television to watch him fight had that? To understand why these people were skeptical of Gatti's suicide requires an appreciation of his mythology. The mythology of a fighter who could do the impossible.

Preternatural

"Never in my mind did I doubt or want to quit or give up."
—Arturo Gatti

Arturo Gatti was pronounced dead Saturday, July 11, 2009, almost two years from the day he retired from the ring. He was only thirty-seven.

So ended a journey that began on April 15, 1972, in Calabria, Italy, a coastal city perched on the toe of the Mediterranean's boot. A journey that took him from Calabria to Montreal, Quebec, to Jersey City, New Jersey, and eventually to Canastota, New York, home of the International Boxing Hall of Fame (IBHOF).

Gatti had been dead nearly four years by the time he was inducted into the Hall of Fame. His daughter, Sofia, was present. "Thank you from my dad," the seven-year-old told the assembly, Gatti's manager, Pat Lynch, giving her a boost so she could reach the microphone. Junior, then only four years old, was there too. "I'm here to see my daddy," he told the *New York Post*, the little boy looking sharp in a black suit and tie, a McDonald's Happy Meal in his hand. He hadn't been invited, a sign of wounds unhealed and perhaps some trepidation on the part of the IBHOF about putting Amanda in the same room as some of her accusers. Amanda sent

Junior anyway. Unable to travel to the United States because of her "current immigration status," Amanda trusted her friend Victoria Purchio to bring her son to the event. Decorum prevailed.

Amanda was upset, however. In her mind, her son was being excluded from a celebration of his father. "She doesn't have a good relationship with his family," said Purchio, "but she was upset they never mailed an invitation to Junior." Amanda let the IBHOF know about it too, writing a letter to them two days before Gatti's induction. The *New York Post* obtained a copy of the letter. It reads: "I know from the bottom of my heart that my late husband would have wanted his son Arturo Gatti Jr. and his wife to attend the induction ceremony and I am deeply saddened by this decision of your organization not to contact me." She continues: "This avoidance is a serious lack of respect towards my late husband, myself, and most importantly Arturo Gatti Jr., who would have been honored to officially participate/attend the induction ceremony this weekend."

Junior was indeed there. Not acknowledged, not on stage like his sister, but at least in the presence of so many who loved his dad.

And everyone loved his dad. Duva recalls how "the night he fought [Floyd Mayweather Jr.] people were walking up to him and congratulating him." Gatti was struck by what to him was undeserved kindness. "Why are they congratulating me? I lost," he wondered. She told him the truth. "Art, they don't care if you lost—they love you." Sadly, "He didn't buy it. He didn't understand why."

"It's a shame he didn't see it," says Duva, of the affection and gratitude the boxing community felt for Gatti, and a "shame he didn't see himself entered into the Hall of Fame."

When it was his turn to speak, Lynch recalled Gatti's doubt about being Hall of Fame worthy. "He always used to say to us, 'Do you think I'm going to be in the Hall of Fame?' I said, 'Of course. They can't stop you from being in the Hall of Fame. You're deserving.' It's just a great celebration."

▼ ▼ ▼

If any fighter seemed deserving of a great celebration, a long retirement, a happy life after boxing, it was Gatti. In the words of boxing photographer Tom Casino, the handsome fighter who made a name for himself lighting Atlantic City's Boardwalk Hall ablaze was "the poster boy of courage and heart," a universally loved prizefighter who reached his mythical status as much through his own blood as through his opponents'.

Finishing his career with a record of 40-9 with 31 knockouts, Gatti never numbered among the best fighters in the world. It was not ring excellence, that proximity to flawlessness, that distinguished "Thunder," that made him beloved. In a blood sport, excellence can—and often does—leave the audience cold. Even artful destruction can bore if delivered with little passion. Rather, it was his limitations and his ability to overcome them that made Gatti an icon. He was a fighter judged less by the outcomes of his fights than by their violence. He had a knack not just for the dramatic but for the nearly impossible, for the superhuman, and because of that he was insulated more than most from the penalty of defeat.

Gatti bled freely over his sixteen-year career, defeaturing his face one bloody round at a time, remaking it into the visage of a fighter who gave utterly of himself for his own reasons, of course, but for the rapt eyes fixed on him too. "Nobody ever said he was the greatest fighter in the world," reflected Gary Shaw, former Main Events Promotions COO, "but they did say he was the most exciting. He was just a joy to watch."

It was an assessment shared by Lou DiBella, the former HBO executive who is now the CEO of DiBella Entertainment. DiBella called Gatti the "Human Highlight Film" because the fighter "had the 'it' factor. He had all of those external things you need to become a star: he tasted his own blood, fought through a shut eye. He was a warrior. People loved him." Indeed, Gatti had the word "WARRIOR" tattooed across his stomach— and he'd earned the right to identify himself as one.

He is best remembered for his trilogy with Micky Ward, and rightly so. But the first Gatti–Ward fight was considered can't-miss because of each man's reputation: Gatti was by then already, in Casino's words, "the ultimate blood and guts warrior."

▼ ▼ ▼

Gatti won his first of two titles when he decisioned IBF junior lightweight champion Tracy Harris Patterson on December 15, 1995, at New York's Madison Square Garden. Patterson, stepson of two-time heavyweight champion Floyd Patterson, was seven years Gatti's junior.

In jumping out to a lead against Patterson, Gatti drew on the boxing skills he could so easily be coerced into abandoning. He dropped Patterson in the second round. Despite that early success, it was the championship rounds that revealed what would soon become quint-essential Gatti. Fatigued, finding himself drawn into exchanges carried more and more by Patterson—who landed an impossible 52 percent of his punches—Gatti looked doomed. In the twelfth, Patterson crashed fist after fist into Gatti's face. Eyes swelled nearly shut, bleeding from cuts, Gatti absorbed Patterson's desperate attempt to salvage his title until the final bell. At the bell, broken as he was, Gatti scaled the ropes in celebration, rightfully expecting to be crowned a champion.

"I wasn't hurt at all," said a jubilant Gatti. Watching Patterson snap the sweat of Gatti's head late in the fight, seeing the damage that had accumulated on the new champion's face—surely he was lying? How could one endure such punishment and not be hurt? But, then, pain is best discerned in behavior, and even as Gatti teetered around the ring he seemed calm. He was in trouble, certainly, but not hurt in the way a person who'd never left the safe side of the ropes might expect. Gatti seemed comfortable in the fire that would soon burn him into boxing's collective consciousness.

▼ ▼ ▼

Patterson may have failed to hurt Gatti, but Wilson Rodriguez did not. Mind you, it wasn't supposed to be that way.

Fresh off his title-winning performance against Patterson, Gatti returned to Madison Square Garden on March 26, 1996. His opponent that night was the unheralded Dominican Wilson Rodriguez. It was only the second HBO Boxing After Dark card, a series that earned a reputation as a proving ground for fighters. At twenty-three, and already an HBO headliner, the Jersey City fighter had made it if not to the pinnacle of the sport, then to a plateau just beneath.

Not that his brain trust believed the journey complete. In the after-glow of Gatti's title-winning performance against Patterson, Gatti's co-promoters, Dino Duva and Russell Peltz, looked to the stars and saw dollar signs. "To my way of thinking," argued Duva, "Arturo is the com-plete package. He's good-looking, he has charisma, he has an exciting style. And he can fight. When you put all that together, you have some-thing truly special."

Gatti had already achieved the kind of success fighters wear them-selves treadless vainly pursuing. This reality was not lost on Lynch. "We were so excited to be on HBO," he told boxing writer Eric Raskin. "HBO was the king of boxing, we thought if we get a contract with them, we'd have it made."

Yes, Gatti had it made, and in the immediate future, he was supposed to be allowed to enjoy it. A new champion is typically granted a soft first defense of his title. This ritual intended to line a fighter and his team's pockets with easy money before returning to the type of challenges befit-ting a champion. Those challenges bring purses commensurate with risk.

Rodriguez, 43-8-3 with 24 knockouts was supposed to fall if not quickly than at least easily. That's why Lynch pushed to secure him as an opponent: "We battled to get Rodriguez as an opponent. HBO wanted us to fight someone else, and as crazy as it sounds in retrospect, we pushed for Wilson Rodriguez, thinking that would be an easier touch for us." Calling the action from ringside, HBO boxing fixture Jim Lampley echoed Lynch's assessment: "When you lack punching power, that makes it tough going against a gun like Gatti." Lampley wasn't wrong, but Lynch? He had miscalculated.

One of the drawbacks for fighters who make it onto platforms like HBO is that their activity drops. Paid handsomely they need no longer maintain an active schedule, often fighting no more than two times a year. In many cases, a fighter's development suffers as a result. Inactivity and weak competition are no crucible. And strangely, all those empty months in a fighter's schedule, all that availability, can make it harder, not easier, to land a marquee opponent. Why deviate from a light schedule and a good living to take more punishment?

Gatti wasn't falling into this trap. He was fighting Rodriguez barely thirteen weeks out from beating Patterson. But that meant his face had yet to heal fully from the abuse it took. A mere thirty seconds into the fight, Rodriguez buried a right hand into Gatti's cheek. The cheek swelled on impact. "It became apparent immediately," reflected Lynch, "that we brought him back too soon after the Patterson fight."

It only got worse for Gatti. The second round brought another swollen eye, this one the product of Rodriguez's sniping jab. Fighting with two swollen eyes was nothing new for Gatti, who'd overcome the same obstacle against Patterson. As he had against Patterson, as he would countless times in his mythical career, Gatti responded by cranking away with power shots. Pressing Rodriguez toward the ropes, Gatti opened up with a left hook and ate a crisp cross-hook combination that dumped him on the canvas. Up at the count of two, Gatti stormed after Rodriguez. "Getting off the floor kind of woke me up." He revealed later, "I got scared when I went down. I didn't even know I was down until I looked around. I said, 'Oh my god, I'm gonna lose the fight.'"

The action was going Rodriguez's way, but the more successful he was the more Lampley's prefight observation figured in the fight.

Rodriguez chopped away at Gatti in the third, but short on firepower and wearing down, he couldn't return him to the mat. As the action heated up, the fight looked more and more like one that Gatti might salvage. Rodriguez had never intended to go to war. That he was on the brink of one was a sign he was losing control.

In the fifth round, the fight turned for the champion. Undeterred by losing a point for a pair of low blows, Gatti fixed his focus on Rodriguez's body and collapsed him with a left hook. "After he dropped him with the body shot," remembered Lynch, "we jumped up, I looked in Rodriguez's eyes, and I knew Arturo had him."

Lynch may have been wrong about Rodriguez being a soft touch, but he was right about him being finished. Gatti stalked Rodriguez throughout the sixth round. If not emboldened by the wilting fighter before him, Gatti appeared at least comfortable in the simplicity of his task: stay close and swing mercilessly. With a minute to go in the round, his left hook found the mark and put Rodriguez down for good. So ended what would be a candidate for Ring Magazine Fight of the Year honors. Gatti would add that award to his resume the following year.

▼▼▼

"This is my career. It's my life." These words weren't Gatti's, and really, had he uttered them they'd have sounded out of character. One of the things that made Gatti so remarkable was the absence of gravitas in his words, the way he could speak plainly, casually, about the kinds of experiences that leave most people speechless. No, they belonged to Gabriel Ruelas, who offered them to Tim Kawakami in an interview for the *Los Angeles Times*. Ruelas was two weeks away from what might very well be his last chance at a world title.

It was the pursuit of a title that kept Ruelas going. He'd won the WBC junior lightweight title three years earlier when he beat Jesse James Leija, but lost it in December 1995, when he was steamrolled by a thirty-seven-year-old Azumah Nelson. Now twenty-seven, and with a record of 44-3 with 23 knockouts, Ruelas seemed to understand his place in boxing and what it would take for him to maintain or improve it. "I love boxing—I want to stay in it for three more years. But I don't want to stay in it without being a champion. I don't. There's no way I'll stay in it," he told Kawakami. Ruelas had turned in three humdrum performances since his uninspired loss to Nelson. Perhaps this hard-line he was taking on his career—like his performances in his recent fights—was a sign that he was still struggling with the fallout of May 6, 1995.

He scored an eleventh-round stoppage of Jimmy Garcia that night. Garcia never recovered. He collapsed in his corner and was rushed to University Medical Center in Las Vegas. Albert Capanna, the operating surgeon, said Garcia died from "initially undetected slow bleeding from a vein in his head, bleeding that probably began during the fight. Pressure on the brain from the excess blood eventually produced brain death." After thirteen days in a coma, Garcia was declared brain dead and his life-support system was turned off. He was only twenty-three years old.

The tragedy crushed Ruelas, who told *Boxing Monthly*'s Jack Welsh, "I wish it was me who died, not Jimmy. . . . He [Garcia] wanted to make some money and buy his family a nice house. He wanted to do things for his people. Me, I'd already done what I wanted to do. So I wish I was in his position instead. Garcia wanted to get married, live better. Well, I have a wife, Leslie, and a ten-week-old son, Diego. I tell people I've already been rich from boxing."

So if anyone understood what danger slipping between the ropes brought, it was Ruelas; if anyone understood how confronting that danger could transform your life, it was Ruelas. "I know more than anybody else how big this fight really is," he told Kawakami. "There is no way I can let it get away." Speaking of the parallels between his first title-winning performance and his shot at Gatti's gold, Ruelas reflected calmly: "Everything just kind of fits in. I did it then and I'll do it better

Dr. Alfred Bowles, who was hired by private investigators to analyze information taken by Brazilian authorities during the investigation into Gatti's death, uses a mock strap as he talks about his findings during a press conference at Global Boxing Gym in North Bergen, New Jersey, on September 7, 2011. *Julio Cortez/ AP/Shutterstock*

Micky Ward and Arturo Gatti look on as Kathy Duva speaks at a press conference to announce what would be Gatti's last fight, a loss to Alfonso Gomez. *Rick Mackler/ Globe Photos*

Arturo Gatti with comedian and actor John Leguizamo at the W Hotel VIP Lounge during Olympus Fashion Week in New York City in 2005. *Djamilla Rosa Cochran/WireImage*

His lip torn, Gatti tries to gather himself after being sent
to the canvas in his fight against Alfonso Gomez. *Al Bello/
Getty Images*

Gatti shares the cover of *The Ring* magazine with Floyd Mayweather Jr. ahead of their fight at Boardwalk Hall in Atlantic City on June 25, 2005. The Ring Magazine *via Getty Images*

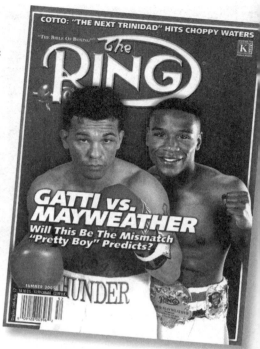

Floyd Mayweather stuns Gatti during their fight. Mayweather won by TKO in the sixth round. *Al Bello/ Getty Images*

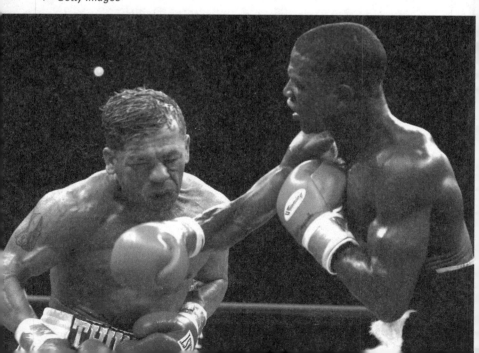

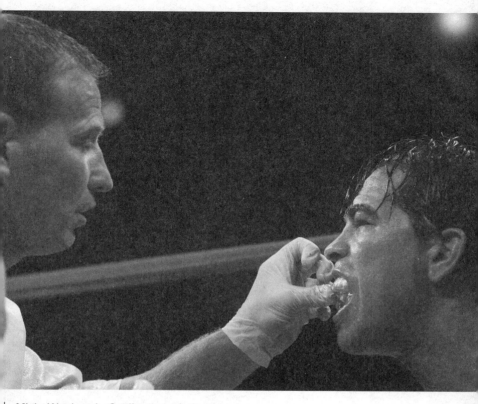

Micky Ward works Gatti's corner during the
Alfonso Gomez fight. *Al Bello/Getty Images*

Gatti makes his way to the ring to face Alfonso Gomez accompanied by Chuck Zito (left) and Micky Ward. *Al Bello/Getty Images*

Gatti celebrates at the end of his 1997 fight against Tracy Patterson. Minutes later Gatti was awarded the IBF super-featherweight world title by unanimous decision. *Al Bello/Allsport*

Micky Ward punches Gatti during their unforgettable first fight, which Ward won by majority decision. The Ring Magazine *via Getty Images*

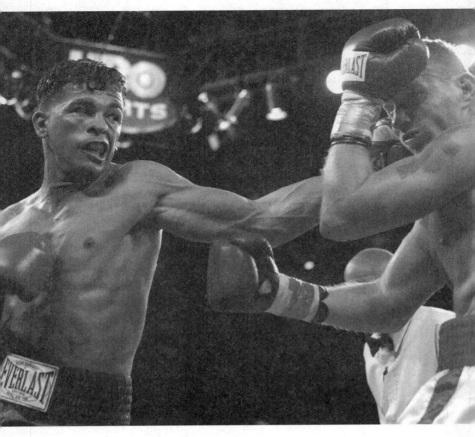

Gatti lands a left hook on Ward in their second
fight en route to winning a lopsided decision.
Al Bello/Getty Images

now because of what I've been through. I've been through the wars." He was on the verge of another one.

▼▼▼

Gatti–Ruelas took place on October 4, 1997, at Caesars Hotel and Casino in Atlantic City. It was the co-feature to Lennox Lewis's defense of his WBC heavyweight title against Andrew Golota. Lewis wiped Golota out in ninety-five seconds, which was for the best because Gatti–Ruelas turned the heavyweight fight into a walkout bout.

Against an opponent with a reputation for eating punches and swelling badly, one could understand why Ruelas started fast. By the second round, he was landing hard uppercuts and hooks on Gatti, but the difference in the two fighters' punches was audible. Ruelas would spin Gatti's head with his best punches, but Gatti responded in kind and stiffened Ruelas's legs with a hook before round's end. His legs back under him, Ruelas continued to throw fight-altering punches while Gatti, unperturbed, waded calmly into this onslaught, thumping his fists off Ruelas's body.

At the end of the second round, trainer Joe Goossen implored Ruelas to be more defensively responsible. "You gotta keep that right hand up more," stressed Goossen, "I don't wanna see you get hit with that fuckin' hook again." There was no avoiding Gatti's hook. What Ruelas had to prove was that he could tax Gatti for landing it.

In the fourth round, he did just that. After losing the opening two minutes to Gatti, who was boxing well, Ruelas ate a cracking hook along the ropes and exploded into action. Gatti, focusing on Ruelas's body, which he found with enticing ease, became a little careless with his guard. Ruelas saw his chance and snapped a series of uppercuts into Gatti's chin, the last of which spun Gatti's head. Wobbled, Gatti backed away with Ruelas in pursuit. But true to form, Gatti sought only enough room to answer back. He met the charging Ruelas with a pair of hooks to the body then traded with Ruelas—who returned doggedly to his right uppercut—until the bell sounded. A Gatti left hook punctuated the round just as the bell sounded to end it.

The punch he was looking for, the punch Goossen had expressed such concern about, was still there for Gatti. And with his eye swelling, a slight smile broke across Gatti's face. It stayed there as he walked woozily to his corner.

While Gatti's corner worked through its invigorating ritual, pouring water on his head and neck, massaging his shoulders with ice, trainer Hector Rocha implored Gatti to be more responsible: "Don't stand in front of the guy! Jab! Move!" pleaded Rocha. "Don't go to war with him! C'mon!" It was good advice, though there was futility in Rocha's tone. Gatti had shown early that he could trouble Ruelas with his jab and, when concerned with such matters, could slip Ruelas's wider punches well. But by then Rocha must have known what Lynch said in an interview with the *New York Times* two years later: "With Arturo there are no easy fights. He is in a battle when he shadowboxes."

Gatti responded to Rocha's instructions by getting off his stool and engaging in what would eventually be named Ring Magazine Round of the Year for 1997.

Ruelas went after Gatti, knowing that the previous round might still be rampaging through Gatti's brain. Again the right uppercut was his choice, and he landed a hellish one less than thirty seconds into the round. Gatti rocked back on his heels, eating leather as Ruelas, both hands churning, walked him down. But he halted his retreat long enough to unload a big left hook that got a tiny stumble out of Ruelas. Ruelas turned unsteadily, opened his arms to Gatti, inviting attrition, and charged. Bleeding under his left eye, Gatti welcomed his opponent's presence, knowing his target by feel. He sunk body shots and left hooks into Ruelas, but Ruelas was undeterred, accepting the immolation that might make amends for Jimmy Garcia. Cracked with a right hand, Ruelas pounded his chest defiantly, then whiplashed Gatti with a pair of uppercuts and drove him across the ring with his follow-up barrage. Tellingly however, he held Gatti when they reached the ropes and continued to hold when Gatti tried to spin away. As Gatti backed to center ring, Ruelas again tried to drape his arms over Gatti instead of punching. Gatti seized the opportunity to unload with body punches, straying conveniently low with an especially evil left hook. Seconds later a right hand and a cross-hook combination put Ruelas down hard.

Goossen had warned him; Goossen knew—"that fuckin' hook." Ruelas was up at the count of eight, but referee Benji Esteves waved the fight off.

Gatti collapsed in his corner seemingly on the verge of tears, though what can be read in a face so misshapen? As the cameras fixed on Ruelas, wrapped in a swirl of care and consolation, Roy Jones Jr. questioned the wisdom of going to war with Gatti. "Why would you go in there and swap punches with a guy who can punch and who is known for the comeback victory?" It seemed a reasonable question to ask considering Gatti's tendency toward the improbable; but, then, what is a fighter supposed to do when he sees his opponent bleeding, swollen, and struggling? The purpose was not to "swap punches" so much as to exploit Gatti's vulnerabilities— the same vulnerabilities that were necessary for a Gatti comeback.

Opponents primed for such exploitation were out there, and they wanted their shots. For now, Gatti, thanks of course to considerable help from an inspired Ruelas, could relax in the glory of earning Ring Magazine 1997 Fight of the Year honors.

▼▼▼

It had been almost six years since Gatti lost, six years since an unheralded Philadelphia fighter named King Solomon confounded the then 6-0 Gatti at the famed Blue Horizon in Philadelphia. But that was about to change.

Angel Manfredy was the first fighter to reacquaint Gatti with defeat. The two met at Convention Hall in Atlantic City on January 17, 1998. Again HBO carried the broadcast. It wasn't Gatti's heart that failed him against Manfredy, but his face, which in retrospect should come as little surprise considering Gatti was barely three months removed from his disfiguring battle against Ruelas.

A wild kid from Gary, Indiana, then the "Murder Capital of America," Manfredy had survived a serious car accident early in his career—back when he was still trying to advance his career while self-sabotaging it with drugs and alcohol—to fight his way to a record of 22-2-1 with 18 knockouts. Manfredy was a good boxer who, like Gatti, fell short of world-class. But nothing about Gatti intimidated Manfredy: not his power, not his toughness, not his mystique. "I called out Gatti after I knocked out [Jorge] Paez," Manfredy told Anson Wainwright for ringtv .com. "I told him what was going to happen before the fight, 'I'm going to knock you down, I'm going to cut you and stop this fight. You're not going the distance.'"

Manfredy made good on his talk. In the opening round, he cut Gatti's left eye with a right hand. It was a bad cut, and Gatti knew it: "At the end of the first round I felt the blood dripping and I knew I was in trouble." Still, Gatti had fought through near blindness before and would do so again on this night. Manfredy was ready for him.

Unlike previous Gatti opponents, Manfredy refused to get greedy. Despite the rapidly worsening cut over Gatti's eye—a cut that, as early as the second round, prompted a visit from ringside physician Dominic Coletta—Manfredy stayed within himself. "I knew they wouldn't stop it, because it's in his hometown," said Manfredy, so he took what was open to him, boxing Gatti effectively from range and loading up only when the opportunity presented itself. Rodriguez had cooperated, Ruelas had cooperated, but Gatti would find no such deal with "El Diablo." With a minute left in the round, Gatti threw a reckless uppercut followed by a pair of left hooks. Manfredy countered the first hook with one of his own and drilled Gatti to the canvas. Up at six, the HBO commentary team encouraged viewers to expect fireworks, the reasoning being that Gatti was at his most dangerous when endangered. But Manfredy would not be goaded into a mistake.

Gatti tried to work himself into the fight in the middle rounds, every punch he landed was cheered on by the crowd. But Manfredy, who fought with a broken hand from the fifth round on, showed a sturdy chin and remarkable discipline—he would not fight outside himself. Fights are not won with toughness: toughness is a quality that allows the other tools in a fighter's arsenal to manifest. For Gatti, these other tools, these complements to his iron volition, had been size and power. But heading into the eighth round, Manfredy had assayed both and remained unperturbed. With ten seconds left in the round, referee Wayne Hedgpeth called a break in the action to have Coletta examine Gatti's eye. Coletta wiped the blood from Gatti's eye; Hedgpeth waved off the fight.

Coletta stopped the fight because Gatti was "fighting with one eye." One eye? Hadn't Gatti fought with one eye to breathtaking results multiple times before? The crowd booed the stoppage, feeling for their adopted son, feeling robbed of the inevitable rally he would have willed into existence for them. Gatti too was sickened by the outcome. "I was cut and that's the only reason I lost the fight," insisted Gatti, "I would have knocked him out in the later rounds."

Despite bringing Manfredy up from junior lightweight, a move that allowed Gatti a significant size advantage and denied Manfredy a chance at a title, despite the broken hand that hampered Manfredy's attack, in Gatti's eyes, and those of his supporters, he fell short against Manfredy in part because "Thunder" had been prevented from channeling his best self. They believed that were Gatti afforded that opportunity there wasn't a fighter in his division who could withstand him. Before the year was over, however, Gatti met the fighter who could.

▼▼▼

Only seven years into his career, people began to wonder openly about what Gatti had left. His battles in the ring and even on the scale, where he fought to keep his body at a weight that could maximize his power, were taking their toll. His behavior beyond the ring was a concern as well, detrimental as it was to his present and future. Describing him as a "nicer version of Jake LaMotta, the Raging Bull," DiBella told the *New York Times* in 1999 that Gatti was "untamed," that "his lifestyle is fairly wild outside the ring, too. If there wasn't prizefighting, he'd be in trouble, because he'd be fighting anyway."

"Arturo has always scared me," continued DiBella, "because Arturo is reckless. He's into having a good time. But sometimes he doesn't think. I don't think Arturo will hurt anyone but himself. He just has a sixth sense for a beef."

The notion that Gatti wouldn't hurt anyone but himself was soon debunked. That "sixth sense" DiBella spoke of was figuring in Gatti's personal life with disturbing regularity. Even with prizefighting as a channel for his destructive inclinations, Gatti was finding his way to trouble. The people closest to him could see it. He was partying with the same abandon he brought to the ring. Staggering out of New York nightclubs, occasionally barreling into friends like his longtime assistant trainer Mike Skowronski's house in the trouble hours, looking to rekindle the fun of an evening that should've ended at last call. Nor did Gatti restrict his drinking to the evening. "When we'd play golf, he'd be drunk by the eighth hole," Skowronski told nj.com.

What's worse, Gatti's drinking led to more than just surprise knocks on Skowronski's door, more than frustrated bartenders and doormen. During an adventurous night in Miami, Gatti and his girlfriend at the time attracted the attention of a hanger-on who persisted in their company throughout the evening. Later that night, misjudging his place with his new friends, this gentleman suggested a threesome. Gatti wasn't thrilled by the offer. As George Kimball wrote for the *Irish Times*, "Arturo's fists were usually his best friend, but in this case they betrayed him: it turned out he had hit the would-be swinger so hard that the telltale marks on Gatti's knuckles perfectly matched the pattern of the staples from the guy's hair implants." In the process of his arrest, Gatti threatened a police officer and had to enter a diversion program to settle the case.

For a wild man like Gatti, this may have been a fairly tame misadventure, but there were more-serious ones too. In another Miami rampage, Gatti was stabbed in the back in a fight over a girl. The story made the newspapers at the time, something that left Gatti deeply ashamed. "I would never do this stuff if my father was alive," he told Skowronski.

In July of 1997, only five days before he was to begin training for the Ruelas fight, Gatti was pulled over at about three in the morning in Union City, New Jersey, for speeding, running two red lights, and then another two red lights with police in pursuit. The chase ended only when a cabbie who was stopped at a red light kept Gatti from driving long enough for another squad car to block the intersection. When Gatti got out of his vehicle, he stumbled before laying on the pavement. He reeked of alcohol and slurred his speech. After he was cuffed, Gatti became violent, threatening to kill the officer by shooting him and then knocking him unconscious (Gatti's scrambled logic here perhaps an indicator of how intoxicated he was at the time). By the end of the ordeal, Gatti had been charged with "assaulting a police officer, resisting arrest, eluding police, making terroristic threats, driving while intoxicated, refusing to take a Breathalyzer test, and several driving violations." And it wasn't the only time Gatti was charged with a DWI; he had his license suspended three times.

Just as new vistas cannot free you from the troubles in your mind, so did Gatti fail to escape his demons in the ring. Quite the contrary. Now physically unfit for the most grueling preparation in sports, Gatti's training suffered. His in-ring performances followed suit. This left him depressed; depression returned him to the very same self-destructive behavior sabotaging his life.

Here his preternatural capacity for violence worked against him. An unfocused, undertrained, uninspired Gatti was even more likely to engage in a firefight if only because he was less capable of doing otherwise. Even were his fights to become less exciting—a reasonable expectation considering the toll of his nightlife—Gatti was still must-see, and so he could put off the hard questions a less exciting, less beloved fighter in decline might have to ask himself. People expected him to struggle, indeed that was the very condition under which he became their fighter, the one that blinked through the blood and took two, three, four, five, six to land one. "You guys know what I'm all about. I come to fight every fight," Gatti told us. And as long as he was living by his code, well, isn't that what we want for ourselves?

▼▼▼

Gatti drank heavily in the aftermath of the Manfredy loss. He was, to the eyes of Skowronski, "depressed . . . just going through the motions." But seven months later, Gatti was back in the ring, once more at Convention Hall in Atlantic City, once more on HBO, this time in a ten-rounder against Philadelphia's "Mighty" Ivan Robinson.

A member of the 1992 U.S. Olympic team, Robinson ran his professional record to 23-0 with 10 knockouts before dropping a unanimous decision to IBF lightweight champion Phillip Holiday in a fight that featured a staggering 990 landed punches. Robinson's comeback train was derailed in his very next fight when Israel Cardona knocked him out in three rounds. He bounced back with two wins against nondescript opposition and after a cut suffered in training that took him out of the running to face Pomona, California's streaking concussionista, Shane Mosley, Robinson was in line for a Gatti fight.

"When we were planning Arturo's next fight, we wanted to get him a good, tough opponent, but at the same time we wanted a relatively easy fight," said Duva. "He was not at his peak. We thought [Robinson] would be a good test and a quality fight for him, but we thought we would win." It was not an assessment shared by Lynch, who repeatedly pushed back against the matchup because of the problems a slick boxer like Robinson could pose for Gatti.

Indeed a fine boxer, an American Olympian when that distinction still mattered, Robinson was nevertheless short on power. The thinking among Gatti's promoter and among bookies (who had Gatti as a 4-1 favorite) was that it was too much to ask of Robinson to box Gatti for ten rounds without succumbing to the bigger puncher. Gatti himself said that Robinson was "bringing a knife to a gunfight," a dig at Robinson's inferior firepower—one that Robinson kept in mind while discharging it.

Robinson might very well have been subsumed had he tried to matador Gatti for thirty minutes, but he had no interest in going slowly and steadily to his fate. "The whole training camp, all I did was box, box, box. But the moment I ran out to the ring," Robinson told *Sporting News*, "I decided I was going to fight him and he was going to have to kill me." He knew he lacked the power to knock Gatti out. Gatti was right. But even if Robinson lacked the power to win by stoppage, the Philadelphia in him wouldn't allow Gatti to speak that truth without penalty. And Robinson was fighting mad. No one expected him to win. He remembers how "when we got to the fight that night, I bumped into Gatti and his team. One of his muscle guys just looked at me and shook his head and started laughing. It pissed me off."

There to be executed, Robinson sprinted to the ring like a prisoner rushing the gallows. At the opening bell, Robinson moved to center ring, dipped left, and uncorked an overhand right that smacked upside Gatti's head. That flash of belligerence wasn't intended to temper Gatti either. Robinson was ready to fight and proved as much throwing a series of sharp combinations in the round. Gatti looked to counter Robinson with hooks, but the waves of leather from Robinson were tidal. Only when Robinson waited or backed to the ropes did Gatti have a chance. There Gatti unloaded on his stationary target, focusing on the body before finishing with a hook to the head. Robinson was frozen by a hook near the end of the round but responded with another volley of punches that drove Gatti to the ropes. It was Gatti, his left eye already swelling, who was trying to hold as the round ended, and Robinson shoved him off before pumping his fist defiantly at a hostile crowd. As long as he was first, Robinson was in control; Gatti himself imparted this lesson to Robinson in the fourth.

It was a round Robinson seemed to take off, and the first of the fight that permitted the HBO commentary team of Jim Lampley, Larry Merchant, and Jones to engage in a conversation. It was a testament to the action of the opening three rounds that much of what they'd said to that point had been reactionary. Robinson spent the round mostly on his toes, relying on his footwork and quicker jab to establish some distance between him and Gatti. But with forty-five seconds left in the round, Gatti caught Robinson backing into a corner and dropped him with a cross behind the ear. A 10-8 round for Gatti could prove crucial given that even the rounds Robinson seemed to win could go against him in Gatti's building.

Robinson fought the fifth round like he was trying to regain some ground. Following his corner's advice, Robinson focused his punches down the middle, throwing quicker, sharper punches inside Gatti's sweeping bombs. If the excitement of the fourth died down some in the following round, it wasn't for a lack of action but for how clearly that action belonged to Robinson. He did well to control Gatti in the sixth too, until with a minute left, he put Gatti in trouble with a left hook and a right hand. Robinson saw his opportunity and unloaded, landing what seemed like dozens of unanswered punches. Sometimes in boxing though, what appears as the path to victory is a mirage. Ruelas had learned that against Gatti, and Robinson was introduced to it too. As Robinson unloaded, Gatti scrambled him with a right hand. A pair of hooks nearly pitched Robinson forward, and while he shook his head defiantly, he surely welcomed the bell. That Robinson threw a punch after it only confirmed that Gatti had treated him in a manner warranting payback.

It appeared that only the most concussive heroics could deliver Gatti the fight. Even still, Robinson got off his stool for the tenth under the impression he needed to win the round if he wanted to have his hand raised. He fought accordingly: his hands a little slower, footwork looser, nevertheless Robinson strafed Gatti throughout the final round. But with fifty seconds left in the fight, Gatti's left hook turned the action again. Robinson stumbled to the ropes with Gatti in pursuit, winging hooks. His legs having left him, "Mighty" struggled to keep upright but he ducked and leaned as best he could to show referee Earl Morton that he deserved to fight on. Another left hook thudded off his head, but Robinson refused to go down. Gatti had exhausted himself in his fury, and Robinson seized the opportunity to snap home a right hand that forced Gatti to hold. With twelve seconds on the clock, Robinson willed himself into action, backing up Gatti with a combination—and again Gatti found a home for his left hook, deboning Robinson's legs with seven seconds left. But Robinson refused to go down. When the scores were read, Robinson was awarded a split-decision win. The victory was his, but Ring Magazine 1998 Fight of the Year honor he would share with Gatti.

Looking back on the fight in 2015, Robinson told *Boxing News*, "there was no way he was going to just come in and beat me up. I fought that fight to get the respect I needed from the fans." Did he succeed? Perhaps the answer to that question matters less than Robinson's perception of it.

▼▼▼

Respect was something Gatti didn't have to worry about. He had just participated in consecutive Ring Magazine Fights of the Year, and even back-to-back losses weren't going to keep Gatti off HBO. He was back four months later, where he dropped a unanimous decision to Robinson. A string of rehab opponents and knockouts followed, which secured Gatti a $1.8 million payday as a comeback opponent for "The Golden Boy" Oscar De La Hoya in 2001. De La Hoya, who'd lost to Shane Mosley in his previous fight, butchered Gatti in five rounds. That beating served as a stark reminder of Gatti's limitations as a fighter (he was neither world-class nor a welterweight), but, perhaps more important, it laid bare how self-destructive Gatti had been. "I was going a little too crazy between fights," he told *ESPN*, euphemizing the kind of behavior that defies happy endings. In the ugly aftermath of the De La Hoya fight, Lynch said Gatti "was totally unsure if he should keep fighting or not." Ex-fighter-turned-trainer Buddy McGirt had the answer.

▼ ▼ ▼

In a 2005 interview with *ESPN*, Lynch said finding McGirt in the somber aftermath of the loss to De La Hoya "was like something sent from God." McGirt, who'd known Gatti since the mid-nineties, when both were training in the New York/New Jersey area, had recently moved to Florida, where he was trying to establish himself training fighters out of the House of Champions Boxing Club & Gym in Vero Beach. He was looking to build his stable. Gatti, who took six months off after the De La Hoya fight, over which time he was frequently exposed to talk about his demise, was ready for a return to the championship mix. McGirt saw what he needed to believe Gatti could get there: "I remember a lot of people telling me I was wasting my time, that he was washed up as a fighter, that he had nothing left," recalled McGirt in an interview with Ray McNulty for *Scripps* Treasure Coast Newspapers, "but I saw something different, maybe because we were both straight shooters and because I had been where he was going. I saw something in him. He still had good reflexes, still had steady legs, still had the attitude. He had all the things you look for in a fighter. And he wanted to come back and show the world. He just needed to rededicate himself."

"You'll win another world title, forget being shot," McGirt told Gatti. They had agreed to work together on a trial basis for a few weeks, but on the second day Gatti called Lynch: "Pat, Buddy is the new trainer." The swiftness of that decision owes much to McGirt's perceptiveness— he assessed quickly both what Gatti had left and what he needed to do to maximize it—but also to the credibility McGirt had earned. He was a former IBF junior-welterweight champion and two-time WBC welterweight champion who knocked out Gatti's older brother, Joe, in 1995. McGirt was elected to the International Boxing Hall of Fame in 2019.

McGirt's message was simple: "You can do one of two things when you leave the gym: You can go back to your hotel and worry about having bruises on your face or you can go play golf because you're not getting hit in the gym." Gatti wanted to play golf, and so he listened to McGirt, who brought Gatti back to boxing, to taking what opponents offered without offering his head in exchange.

In his first fight under McGirt, in January of 2002, this more-controlled version of Gatti blasted out former IBF junior-welterweight champion, Terron Millett, in four one-sided rounds. Granted, Millett was plenty worn by that point, but he'd engaged in none of the wars Gatti had. Besides, that Gatti won wasn't the point; rather, it's that he did so easily. He fought on his toes, sticking his jab and looking for counters. Of course, his face still swelled—Gatti was never going to be slick, and the skin under his eyes was liable to puff up from a camera flash. But this preservative style not only afforded Gatti the liberty to contemplate his attack but to enjoy the process. Millett came undone in the fourth, the victim not of a desperate hook thrown by a blinded fighter but by a sharp cross hidden behind a double jab—a simple, basic attack out of keeping with Gatti's reputation as a warrior, yes, but one that could spare him the penalty of earning that distinction.

But McGirt's value extended beyond its ring dividends. By prolonging Gatti's career, he was saving the fighter from self-destructive behavior. There was less time for trouble with a rejuvenated career to commit to, and perhaps less interest in it as well. And here it is worth considering what threats lay waiting for Gatti in retirement. What would he do when the discipline of the gym, the expectations of his fans, the desire to compete were gone? Where would all that penchant for living life to the fullest focus itself?

For now, though, Gatti was back. Four months later, he was back to Gatti. He can thank "Irish" Micky Ward for that.

▼ ▼ ▼

In one sense, the Millett fight showed what Gatti was capable of and what he had left. He was capable of something other than self-immolation in a boxing ring. Provided his opponents allowed him to commit to a cooler, more controlled strategy, Gatti the revitalized boxer might fight effectively for years to come. But no one drawn to Gatti the fighter considered his potential in such terms. For the people who tuned in to watch him fight, who filled the seats in the arenas where he performed, what Gatti was capable of was a spectacle at the threshold of human suffering. What he had left? This quantity was measured in the number of times he might return to that threshold. In this sense, it was Ward, not Millett, who laid bare what Gatti might still achieve in the ring.

Ward, then 37-11 with 27 knockouts was, like Gatti, a fighter whose reputation could not be gleaned from his record. He was a career journeyman who worked as a road paver to supplement his ring earnings. But Ward refused to carry himself like an opponent. In 1997, Top Rank Promotions paid Ward $10,000 ostensibly to pad the record of undefeated prospect Alfonso Sanchez. Sanchez had knocked out fifteen of his sixteen opponents and was expected to continue that trend against Ward. The bout went according to script for six rounds as Sanchez pulped Ward, dropping him with a left uppercut in the fifth. Ward could do little but bang his fists in frustration and keep his guard up. There was little evidence the fight would change, and thus little reason to let it continue. Before the seventh, referee Mitch Halpern came to Ward's corner: "Show me something or I'm stopping the fight."

With about ninety seconds left in the round, Ward landed a left hook to Sanchez's body. A quick, compact shot, it barely registered amid the torrent of punches Sanchez had thrown, but Sanchez stopped throwing for just a moment—and Ward knew why. "I heard him grunt," Ward said afterward. Seconds later Ward whipped another hook into Sanchez's body. This time the effect was undeniable. Sanchez collapsed in agony while Halpern administered a perfunctory count.

Two years later, Ward was again fighting for his career, this time in a crossroads bout against "Showtime" Reggie Green for ESPN's *Friday Night Fights*. A meager crowd of two thousand was on hand at the Icenter in Salem, New Hampshire, to watch the Lowell, Massachusetts, fighter once more beat back irrelevance. Green dominated the bout early, nearly finishing Ward in the third. But with the fight slipping away, Ward committed fully to his body attack and Green wilted. In the tenth, thirty seconds from victory, Green had to be rescued by the referee.

Ward's reputation for heroics and left hooks reached its then-pinnacle less than a year before he and Gatti squared off. Again, Ward was headlining *Friday Night Fights*, this time against Emanuel Augustus (then Burton), a Chicago-born journeyman worlds better than his 24-17-4 record indicated. Together, they produced Ring Magazine 2001 Fight of the Year, and again, it was Ward's left hook to the body that sealed the win for him when he dropped Burton with it in the ninth round.

Ten months later, on May 18, 2002, Gatti and Ward stood across the ring from each other at the Mohegan Sun Casino in Uncasville, Connecticut. Every one of the 6,254 people in attendance, every one of the people who tuned in to HBO "expected a good fight" said Hall of Fame trainer and analyst Emanuel Steward. They got a legendary one instead.

▼▼▼

Gatti's composed performance against Millett didn't go unnoticed by Ward and his half-brother/trainer, Dick Eklund. It was a version of the "Human Highlight Film" the brothers had little interest in solving. "I don't want to be at the end of his punches," Ward told *ESPN*. "If I could get him into his old style that would be to my advantage." Ward figured he would be behind on the cards if Gatti boxed from the outside, and he was tired of having to war his way back into fights, tired of having a physician's discretion deny him a chance at victory (sound familiar?). To improve his chances, so reasoned Ward and Eklund, Ward would have to revert Gatti back into a brawler, engage him at his most dangerous. It was a gutsy play. Despite spending most of his career below junior welterweight, Gatti was bigger than Ward, he hit harder, he moved better, he was six years younger than the thirty-six-year-old Ward, and while Gatti had been through countless wars, he wasn't coming off a grueling Fight of the Year. None of this was lost on Ward. And none of it phased him. "This is do or die," he said.

And so it was Ward who started maliciously, winging a huge left hook in the opening seconds and looking to land power shots. Following McGirt's plan, Gatti boxed almost lithely in contrast to the wide-stanced creeping of Ward. But halfway through the round, Gatti planted his feet and opened up with a combination punctuated by a pair of left hooks—and just like that, Ward was bleeding. His response? Bang his gloves together, wipe the cut, and walk Gatti down. Gatti teed off on Ward because he had the opportunity too, yes, but also because he had to. The ring was shrinking already, and that favored Ward.

By the third round, as if by Ward's will alone, a fight broke out. Gatti tried to box, but Ward landed enough well-placed body shots to make escape less appealing than retaliation. And so Gatti hurled away with hooks and uppercuts while Ward leaned into him, tapping him with light left hooks to the head before ripping into his body. Gatti had shimmied at the end of round two, pleased with himself. When the bell rang to end round three, however, it was Ward who offered a little celebration, tapping Gatti on the head before heading to his corner. The crowd roared its approval.

The crowd got more of what it wanted in the middle rounds. That characteristic of all truly great fights—drastic and pronounced swings of momentum—figured throughout as the fighters retaliated to every flash of their own vulnerability. But it was Ward—bleeding from his eye, his nose, his mouth, dropped in the fourth by a low blow that cost Gatti a point—who seemed happiest immersed in this mutually assured destruction. It was Ward who banged his gloves inviting punishment, Ward who punched through the timekeeper's bell, Ward who fought like a man with everything to lose.

For his part, Gatti obliged, but his violence was reactionary; there was a hesitation to it. Unlike Ward, Gatti's first step after a salvo was backward. He never shied from the heat, but then he didn't step gladly onto the coals either. He had wanted to win another way and Ward had refused him that course. Watching Gatti brought to mind a line from Macbeth:

> I am in blood
> Stepp'd in so far that, should I wade no more,
> Returning were as tedious as go o'er.

Still, after getting torched in the fifth round, Gatti found room to move in the sixth. Ward appeared to tire a little. After the seventh, another strong Gatti round, Eklund urged Ward to "bang the shit out of him," adding, "If you're gonna be a punching bag, I'm not gonna let this go." Ward was no punching bag in the eighth and hurt Gatti with another hook to the body near the end of the round. The momentum, however, had swung in Gatti's favor. Ward would need to swing it back; Gatti would have to deny that swing. And that struggle produced Ring Magazine Round of the Year for 2002.

Fifteen seconds into round nine, Ward sunk the left hook he'd wanted all night. Gatti dropped his hands, backed away, and folded to a knee. Referee Frank Cappuccino started to count, showing his fingers to a grimacing Gatti, who stood at the count of nine. Ward tore after him, swinging tirelessly as Gatti stumbled across the canvas. But after thirty seconds of near helplessness, Gatti channeled his greatest self, planted his feet, and swung back. Having worn himself out trying to end the fight, Ward was stalled by the return fire coming. But rather than use this as an opportunity to escape, Gatti doubled down, ripping into Ward with an uppercut-hook combination.

And then the unthinkable: Ward took a backward step.

Gatti encouraged another as he drove straight through Ward's guard, forcing the tiring fighter to the ropes, drilled him with a pair of body shots, and seared him with a cross. The Herculean effort took its toll on both fighters, and Gatti fell into a clinch. When Cappuccino separated them, the momentum swung again as Ward cracked Gatti with a pair of right hands and another left hook to the body. Gatti rocked back, and as he leaned forward, Ward snapped his head with an enormous uppercut, then bored into the wilting fighter as Gatti sagged along the ropes. With thirty-five seconds left in the round, Gatti looked finished, and Cappuccino drew himself to an intervening distance. "You can stop it any time!" roared Lampley from ringside. "Arturo Gatti is out on his feet!" Cappuccino, however, knew who he was officiating, knew he was in the presence of the impossible, and so he let ride to its conclusion a round that belonged to the fighters.

There was, of course, no way for the tenth to live up to its predecessor, but that was hardly a criticism. Few rounds in a lifetime come close to providing the kinds of thrills round nine delivered. The punishment ended with the final bell, and Ward was announced the winner by majority decision.

The rematch took place on November 23 of that year. Gatti won easily, coasting to victory after dropping and badly hurting Ward in the third. The final bout in the trilogy unfolded the following June. Gatti was again in complete control until he hurt his right hand landing an uppercut on Ward's hip. His weapons halved, Gatti, though he managed a decision victory, was once more was pushed to the brink by the man he would forever be linked to.

▼▼▼

At a time when the best fighters in the world rarely fought three times a year, Gatti and Ward fought three times in thirteen months. And twice produced the Ring Magazine Fight of the Year.

The mark Gatti and Ward left on each other over those three fights was something neither fighter could forget. In an interview with Chris Jones for *Esquire*, Gatti itemized some of what made up that mark. In their rematch, Gatti hit Ward so hard and so often the titanium plate in Gatti's surgically repaired right hand came loose. A punch to Ward's hip broke that same hand in their third fight. And then there was what Gatti referred to lovingly as his "Micky Ward lump": a cyst on his ribcage, a keepsake from their first fight. Ward had his scars too. The punch that dropped Ward in their second fight broke Ward's eardrum. The punishment Gatti gave in their third fight retired Ward, leaving him with permanent tunnel vision.

Still, a friendship was born of all those brutal rounds, one rooted in more than a mutual affinity for war and its wounds. Gatti and Ward had developed a trust. There may be no more trustworthy person in your life than the one who tries to raze you to the ground. You know where you stand with that person. That person's intentions are clear. "Anytime you go thirty rounds with a guy, try to kill each other," said Ward, explaining the strength of his friendship with Gatti, "and have the most respect for each other, no one understands that, but guys who have been to war understand it."

So when someone pulls back the dividing curtain in the hospital room you've been sent to because you can't hear out of your left ear, or because you can't feel your right hand, and you see the person responsible for your suffering smiling and wishing you well, you've made a friend for life. Ward remembers that visit in the hospital. "I was lying in a hospital bed and the doctor treating me says, 'There's someone who wants to see you,' and pulls the curtain back and there's Gatti. He looked at me and

51

asked if I was OK." Asked about Gatti while at a racetrack in Toronto, Ward said: "I tried to kill him in the ring, not literally kill him but beat him any way I could, and I miss him like a brother."

It's no wonder that Gatti had Ward train him for what proved to be his final fight in 2007.

▼▼▼

Gatti lost that night, knocked out in seven rounds by Alfonso Gomez. But the loss did nothing to diminish his legacy. By then Gatti had become a myth incarnate, a fighter for whom, in his own words, giving up was impossible. It isn't difficult to understand then why so many people refused to believe he killed himself and, subsequently, why they couldn't understand how Amanda, whatever the explanation from Brazilian law enforcement, could be released. Suicide, if interpreted as an ultimate act of resignation, was a form of giving up one could not return from. Surely Gatti, so the reasoning might go, who never gave up in the ring would never give up on life.

Wittgenstein once remarked that mythological explanations have an appeal because they say that an event is "a repetition of something that has happened before. And when people do accept or adopt this, then certain things seem clearer and easier for them." Could it be that Gatti's mythology—born of his superhuman capacity to fight, to persist in the face of profound suffering—was butting up against a reality that imposed some limits on that mythology's ability to explain him? Did Gatti's suicide meet with such strong resistance because it was a lie, or because it threatened to disgorge a truth that forced a reevaluation of Gatti and what the world knew of him? Might it make a fighter that seemed to belong to the world (considering how freely he gave himself to it) no longer the world's? No longer ours?

Confrontation

"Everything is what it is, and not another thing."
—Bishop Butler

A lready buried by his family in Montreal, Gatti was celebrated at a mass at St. John the Baptist Church in Jersey City. Among the more than six hundred people present to say their goodbyes were actor Mickey Rourke; fighters Mickey Ward, Tracy Patterson, and Chuck Wepner; and Chuck Zito, the former president of the New York chapter of the Hells Angels. An unmistakable figure, Zito could be seen accompanying Gatti on his ring walks. This eclectic group was proof of Arturo's charm, of the magnetic quality of the fighter who loved so easily. Moreover, it was a testament to his mythological capacity for violence, one that could transfix even the abolitionists.

Lou DiBella brought the attendees to their feet when he told them, "God knows that Arturo Gatti never quit in his life. Arturo Gatti did not quit in Brazil." Skepticism about Gatti's suicide, and, by extension, Amanda's innocence, ran high. In that grieving echo chamber on the corner of Brooks Place and John F. Kennedy Boulevard, that skepticism's mournful expression was amplified. Only a few hours earlier, the Brazilian authorities had changed Gatti's cause of death from homicide to suicide and ordered Amanda's release from police custody. It was an unpopular decision among the attendees, people who had gathered to celebrate a man who loved life—a man who wouldn't quit.

▼▼▼

No, Gatti wouldn't quit. The news from Brazil did nothing for his friends' suspicions. Skowronski was incredulous, telling Deadspin's Dashiell Bennett, "Absolutely a hundred percent couldn't ever see him commit suicide. He loved life. If he was going to kill himself, he would have called and said goodbye to me."

The image of Gatti as a man happy in the languor of retirement was chorused by his closest friends and family. Asked about the mysterious details of Gatti's death, his nemesis-turned-friend and trainer, Ward, said: "I just can't see him taking his own life. It's just not him. Everything in life was goin' good for him." Like Ward, a close friend of the Gatti family, Ivano Scarpa, thought the suicide explanation impossible. "Nobody believes whatsoever that there's even a one percent chance of suicide," said Scarpa. "He lived his life to the fullest." Count Gatti's ex-fiancée Rivera among the skeptics too. She called the suicide explanation "bullshit," saying Gatti "could get a little crazy, he was a little superstitious, but suicidal? Never. He was a free spirit who loved life." Montreal boxer Howard Grant, a close friend of Gatti's, was even stronger in his refusal of the suicide verdict, telling *CTV News*: "I will go to my grave, I will put my hand on the bible, and tell God to strike me down, there is no way Arturo killed himself."

Speaking of Gatti's suicide years later, Kathy Duva concedes that she "can't look into someone's soul and tell what they can do" but cannot bring herself to accept the explanation for Gatti's death. "The thing that makes me not believe is that if he was going to take his life he wouldn't take it that way." This tempered doubt is in stark contrast to the dogmatic assertions of her fellow suicide skeptics. She moves in from the poles of murder and suicide to a position that exhibits greater nuance. Duva continues: "He had access to drugs, he might take drugs, he might drive his car into a wall. He wouldn't hang himself with his wife's purse strap. I knew him well enough to know that. How he did it? There were easier ways, less confounding ways."

Gatti had his dark moments and they are well-documented. But Duva encourages a shift in focus from the perplexity of the act itself to its logistical peculiarities. "Something sudden—I can buy that. But this was a plan. How did he pull it off in that state? And the wife's purse strap seems like a message. Somebody did it and I don't think it was him. I mean, why would you hang yourself from so high? You don't need to do that."

The timing seemed odd too. "He had gotten his permanent residence," remembers Duva, "he planned to become a U.S. citizen. I had written a letter to help him, there were some concerns about how this retired boxer was going to earn a living in the U.S." Upon getting the good news, Gatti came into Duva's office. "He was so happy, he thanked me. Now, you're so depressed you can kill yourself but you're making plans like that?"

Duva knows the psychology of the men she works with, their proclivity for risk-taking and self-destruction, but "I don't believe in coincidences," she says, "and I see this as a series of unbelievable coincidences."

That is Duva's opinion now, and it was that of Main Events ten years before. Through spokeswoman Ellen Haley, the promotional outfit made clear their position on his death, saying "we do not believe that he took his own life," adding: "We believe that once the results of that investigation are revealed, the truth will come to light and justice will be done." Yes, while the investigation may have been completed in the eyes of Brazilian authorities, in the United States and Canada, there were people who believed further digging was in order.

▼▼▼

No one was more steadfast in his suspicions about Gatti's suicide than Pat Lynch. He refused that explanation from the very beginning, and no investigation conducted in a foreign country was going to convince him otherwise. At the memorial, when asked about Gatti's death, Lynch remained unshaken: "No way, in a million years, would Arturo Gatti commit suicide." And Lynch was willing to prove it. In his opinion, the Brazilian investigation was pathetic. At the memorial, he vowed to pursue a full investigation into Gatti's death. In fact, the wheels of that investigation were in place even before Gatti was determined to have died by his own hand. Lynch had retained Brazilian lawyers in the hopes of again putting Amanda on trial, either in Canada or Brazil. What he was short on was evidence that justified reopening the case. For that, he turned to Paul Ciolino and Joe Moura.

Ciolino, who died in 2017, had the bearing of a gumshoe. His thick eyebrows, bulldog's jowls, and heavy Chicago accent gave him a knowing, intimidating mien. He spoke forcefully, using a mix of legal jargon and street slang that gave you the impression he was as comfortable on the stand as he was on the street corner—and unlikely to slip up on either. In this respect, he was perfect for television. You might have seen him on television too. Ciolino, who Dan Rather once called "one of America's top five investigators," had at one time or another appeared on FOX, MSNBC, CNN, ABC, NBC, and CBS. He didn't just look the part though. Before operating his own business—the Paul J. Ciolino and Associates International Forensic Consortium—Ciolino worked in the Department of Child and Family Services for the state of Illinois as the lead homicide and mass molestation advisor. While there he obtained over two hundred written confessions pertaining to homicides and sexual assaults. Ciolino was also the first private investigator to be certified as a forensic criminal profiler.

That high-profile case caught the attention of Lynch, who had seen Ciolino's work on the Amanda Knox case for the CBS investigative journalism show *48 Hours*. Lynch was thrilled with the findings of the private investigation too, saying that the work Ciolino and Moura put in was a "gift from God." That work consisted in hiring "two of the biggest names in forensic pathology, an expert in forensic animation, an expert in human movements, a retired FBI agent, a doctor who is an injury and causation medical doctor and an expert in injuries, and a criminal profiler and crime scene expert." The plan was to use police photos to physically and digitally reconstruct the crime scene to determine whether Gatti could have hung himself. The last two members of the team, though, make clear the real purpose of the investigation: Ciolino and Moura intended to prove Gatti was murdered.

▼▼▼

For one day, September 7, 2011, Global Boxing Gym in North Bergen, New Jersey, was converted into a pressroom. The ring lay empty, the weights silent, the bags—heavy, speed, double-end—were still. Listening and instruction, the cornerstones of any boxing gym worth its salt, would fill the day. The sweet science was not the subject, however—murder was. A makeshift dais for ten was arranged ringside, along with a lectern and a projection screen. A few feet away, rows of folding chairs supported members of the press on hand to hear the findings in what was called a million-dollar investigation into the death of Arturo Gatti.

"Ladies and gentlemen," said Ciolino, his voice rising, pronunciation becoming intentionally percussive, "I would come back from the grave to prove this case as a homicide. Arturo Gatti was murdered. He didn't commit suicide. He was murdered plain and simple."

The team looked at Gatti's position on the floor as a reason to question the veracity of the initial investigation. The Brazilian autopsy concluded that Gatti hanged himself from the staircase and hung there for hours until the strap eventually broke, dropping Gatti where Amanda found him on the floor. But Gatti was found under the stairs, which was puzzling. Using a program to digitally re-create the crime scene, the investigators dropped a dummy the same size as Gatti from where he had hung. According to Ciolino, a thousand tries later the dummy had yet to land under the stairs. It was the opinion of Alfred Bowles, the expert in human movements recruited by Ciolino for the investigation, that Gatti could not have landed under the stairs if he hung himself. He had to have been strangled by someone else, or his body would have had to have been moved, or both.

The purse strap was another point of suspicion. According to the Brazilian investigation, Gatti used the strap—which had both blood and skin on it—to hang himself. Strangely, though, the strap was found a few feet from Gatti's body, not around his neck (something confirmed by police photos of the crime scene). For Ciolino, this left some holes in the conclusion that Gatti indeed hanged himself with the purse strap. "There's no implement around his neck," he said in an interview for Canadian true-crime series *The Fifth Estate*. "So if he hung himself, who the hell knows how he hung himself?" Ciolino figured that the Brazilian police saw the marks on Gatti's neck, saw the bloody purse strap, and concluded Gatti hung himself with it. But even if that conclusion appeared logical, Ciolino argued further evidence was needed to establish it—evidence the Brazilian investigation failed to gather. Had they wanted to firmly establish the purse strap—which was not only not around Gatti's neck but some distance away—as the implement in Gatti's hanging, Ciolino said the Brazilian authorities needed to test the strap. Had Gatti used the strap it would've picked up metal scrapings from the railing. What's more, the metal on the strap would have had wood and varnish from the stairs on it. No such testing was conducted, however.

Then there was Gatti's head wound. It was Ciolino's opinion that Gatti suffered that injury while being rendered unconscious so that he could be easily strangled. One of the reasons Ciolino forwarded this idea was the peculiar absence of blood at the crime scene. There was no blood on the floor where Gatti was determined to have hung himself, no blood on Gatti's back, though he was shirtless when found, and no blood on the stool Gatti used to hang himself. The only blood found was pooled around his head and on two towels that the Brazilian investigation strangely never analyzed.

So who struck him? Who strangled him? The answer was obvious. If he didn't strike or strangle himself, and no one else entered the room, the only other person who could have done it was his wife. "It's got to be Amanda," concluded Ciolino.

The investigation that started with the intention of clearing Gatti's name claimed to be a success. But did Ciolino, Moura, and their team hit the mark? Or did they fire an arrow and draw a bull's-eye around where it landed?

▼▼▼

There were reasons to doubt the conclusions of the private investigators. For one, in re-creating Gatti's hanging, they hung a dummy by wrapping a leather strap around one of the balusters that supported the handrail of the staircase. This meant the strap was on a diagonal, hanging out over the edge of the staircase and around Gatti's neck. But the Brazilian investigation said the body had been hung from the handrail itself, which means the strap hung vertically. This difference was significant. It could have changed how Gatti's body fell and thus where it came to rest. Gatti might very well have ended up under the stairs had he hung himself from the railing. There was also the fact that some of the crime-scene photos the investigation team was working with had been taken after items in the room had been moved. In particular, a stool found under the stairs was initially positioned by Gatti's feet, a location Bowles concedes could have altered the results of his experiments.

Ciolino's criticism of the Brazilian investigation's treatment of the purse strap was also less damaging than it appeared to be. Fibers found on the railing matched fibers found on the strap. What's more, these fibers were found on the railing, where Gatti, according to the Brazilian authorities, hung himself—and not on the baluster Ciolino's investigation hung their dummy from. There were also marks in the wood of the staircase that matched the shape of the metal clasps on the strap, proving that Gatti did not hang himself from the baluster.

Of course, Amanda might still have strangled Gatti and then hung him to stage a suicide. Where Gatti was ultimately hanged from did not eliminate the possibility that he was murdered. Amanda would have had to overpower him, however, a feat her lawyer and her family had dismissed as preposterous. Ciolino argued that Amanda could have struck Gatti and rendered him unconscious before strangling him. That would explain the wound Gatti had on the back of his head. "When you're unconscious, you're not the Incredible Hulk, you're a dead piece of meat laying on the floor. And a twelve-year-old could strangle you in five seconds," he told *The Fifth Estate*. Forced imagery aside, the problem for Ciolino's argument was that there was no forensic evidence to support it: no weapon, no blood spatter, nothing in the hotel room to suggest Gatti had hurt his head there.

That shortage of forensic evidence might best be explained by the taxi driver who drove Gatti and Junior back to the hotel after Gatti fought the mob. While eyewitness accounts say Gatti fought his attackers like a man possessed, there was no escaping their rage unscathed. Gatti had knocked Amanda to the ground in public, in front of his child, with such force that her injuries were photographed by police, with such force that a group of strangers were driven to attack him while he was in the care of his infant son. Mobs are emboldened by their own actions, and the violence Gatti suffered at the hands of that mob may have had less to do with justice than with power. Still, the incident is proof that there were real problems in Gatti's marriage, the kind of problems that Amanda couldn't euphemize or downplay. She may have wanted to protect the memory of her husband, she may have wanted to depict their marriage as being better than it was (it's easy to remember the good times when the bad ones cannot return) but that night the Gatti marriage was in a state of crisis.

Gatti too was in a state of crisis. The taxi driver that picked him up said Gatti bled heavily in the cab. "I look in the backseat and saw there was blood on the backseat," the driver remembered. "It was a lot. The whole headrest was stained with blood."

For seemingly every question raised by the private investigation, there was an answer. But the day after the private investigators presented their findings in North Bergen, Pernambuco's state prosecutor's office told the Associated Press that they were investigating the Gatti case again and might ask for the private investigators' findings. Jaques Cerqueira, a spokesperson for Brazilian prosecutor Paula Ismail, said that murder charges could be brought against Amanda in light of what this new look at the case revealed, though there was also the chance that the suicide verdict would be upheld. All the while, a nasty civil suit over Gatti's estate was unfolding.

▼ ▼ ▼

Lynch's investigation was more than forensic because it was motivated by judgments of character. Ciolino had done his best to turn room 6305 into a crime scene because Gatti would never kill himself and, therefore, Amanda was capable of murder. In court, the burden of proof lay with the prosecution. But to prove her innocence in the court of public opinion, Amanda had to do more than let the justice system run its course; she had to overcome an ironclad public perception about her late husband: that he refused to quit.

There was evidence, though, that Gatti might not be as resolute in the face of life's challenges as he had been in the face of men's fists. Pain in the ring has an end, and very often that end saw Gatti's hands raised. It has a ceiling conceivably, too, though there was little evidence Gatti was familiar with his—and if he knew his pain threshold, little proof he couldn't ignore it. Pain in the ring? You can appreciate its function, its value. You know your opponent is susceptible to it, and that however much you both may hurt, you can put the pain behind you after the bell. Pain dissipates, heals, and in its retreat is replaced by the flush of health and power that allows you to take it on anew. You are better for your pain.

But not all pain is like that, and there were signs that Gatti's resolve trembled a bit in response to the hurt you don't stitch up or hide behind Ray-Bans. No longer a fighter, was "Thunder" nevertheless suffering the price of being one?

▼▼▼

Concern about Chronic Traumatic Encephalopathy (CTE) has picked up in recent years. This condition, where a person's brain degenerates as a result of brain injury, looms monstrously over sports—and their leagues—where such injury is common. CTE's presence is all the more monstrous for its mystery. How many head injuries are enough to cause CTE? No one can say. How severe must those injuries be? That too is unknown. When do the symptoms of CTE manifest? There is no set period. What's worse, while there have been some encouraging advances in CTE detection, there is as yet no way to diagnose it in living people. If people fear the unknown, CTE might turn their blood cold.

And what science does know is no less frightening. Neuropathologist Ann McKee investigated this mysterious threat. The results of her 2017 study were published in *JAMA: The Journal of the American Medical Association*. McKee examined the brains of 202 deceased football players, their ages ranging from twenty-three to eighty-nine. Of the players in the study, 111 of them played in the NFL, and of those, 110 exhibited signs of CTE. Of those players, forty-four were linemen. These players are typically exposed to the repeated, though seemingly benign, blows that are more likely to result in CTE than their concussive counterparts. It is easy to see how CTE could pervade boxing, where blows both benign (relatively speaking) and concussive are part of the bloody desiderata. In a nod to the importance of CTE research to boxers, Mickey Ward, the man famous for warring thrice with Gatti, intends to donate his brain and spinal column to Boston University's Chronic Traumatic Encephalopathy (CTE) Center.

CTE is known best by its symptoms, which, according to the Mayo Clinic, include depression, impulsive behavior, emotional instability, substance abuse, and suicidal behavior. Gatti exhibited these symptoms throughout his career, and with greater intensity in his retirement. That doesn't mean he had CTE, and, even if he did, it is now too late to know for sure. But there is hardly a better candidate for CTE than the generation's foremost expert in gloved attrition. How likely was it that Gatti suffered the neurological fallout of a life defined by head trauma? How likely is it that it ultimately killed him?

▼▼▼

That Gatti suffered from CTE is an easy, but admittedly speculative, conclusion to reach. It is rooted in Gatti's behavior, like so many of the explanations for how his life ended. This much can be said, at least: Gatti was a prime candidate for the condition, one that could make his impossible death sensible (even logical) and, most important, of his own doing. Evidence that Gatti was struggling with his mental health began to surface late in his life. Court documents filed in 2006 contained testimony from a former girlfriend who said that while living with Gatti the previous year, he had "attempted suicide by overdosing on cocaine, alcohol, and prescription drugs." Records of the incident from Christ Hospital in Jersey City describe Gatti as unresponsive and indicated he tested positive for cocaine and alcohol. Those same records show a doctor's request that Gatti undergo a psychiatric consultation, and in child support documents Erika Rivera called the incident a suicide attempt.

Lynch himself acknowledged that Gatti struggled a bit with drugs. He sought help for his friend and told Gatti he had some concerns about the fighter's substance abuse. But Lynch pushed back against the idea that

Gatti's problems were severe. He doesn't believe Gatti could have accomplished what he did in his career if "Thunder" had a serious substance abuse problem. How else to explain him passing all of those drug tests? Still, Gatti's struggle with drugs is corroborated by Costa, who said the fighter developed an addiction in treating ring injuries. "He got addicted to painkillers—Percocet, Vicodin, Oxys . . . coke. He was just not himself." Gatti was still a teenager when Costa met him, so when he said that Gatti was not himself, he recognized this change against the backdrop of the same Gatti who everyone knew. In that contrast, there is room to question whether the image of Gatti that made suicide so out of character for him wasn't itself a mischaracterization. Even Joe Gatti, who once stood with his family in the belief that Amanda was a murderer, eventually accepted what he believed was the truth about his brother's condition. In a painful interview for *48 Hours*, Joe told host Erin Moriarty, "I just hate to say it, but it came to this, that people need to know the truth. He was on drugs. He was on painkillers. And he was an alcoholic." Asked if he believed Gatti took his own life, Joe responded, "I believe it, I believe it. That night in Brazil, he found himself in a dark place."

He'd been in dark places before. Costa recalls the time a distraught Gatti walked into his New Jersey bar looking for a gun. "He says, 'Please give me my [Costa's] gun.' I was afraid." Recognizing his friend's distress, Costa urged him to seek psychiatric help. Gatti responded by making a gun with his hand, telling Costa, "This is what I'm gonna do," and shoving the pretend barrel in his mouth. "I had my gun there but I told him I don't have my gun," admitted Costa. "I believe if I gave him my gun that night, he would probably blow his head off right in front of me. That's how bad he was."

▼▼▼

"No one, nobody alive, except Amanda, will ever tell you that Gatti was ever suicidal at any time in his life. Never, not one time." These are

Arturo Gatti hammers Micky Ward during their brutal third fight. Gatti ended the trilogy with a unanimous decision win. *Al Bello/Getty Images*

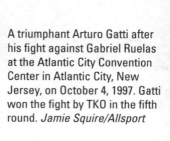

A triumphant Arturo Gatti after his fight against Gabriel Ruelas at the Atlantic City Convention Center in Atlantic City, New Jersey, on October 4, 1997. Gatti won the fight by TKO in the fifth round. *Jamie Squire/Allsport*

Champion again. Arturo Gatti after beating Gianluca Branco for the WBC junior-welterweight world title at Boardwalk Hall in Atlantic City on January 4, 2004.
Ed Mulholland/WireImage

The press conference at Global Boxing Gym in North Bergen, N.J. on September 7, 2011. Investigators revealed findings that disputed Gatti's alleged suicide. *Associated Press*

Amanda Rodrigues is escorted by police officers after being arrested in Recife, Brazil, on Sunday July 12, 2009. *Associated Press*

Amanda Rodrigues is released from a womens' prison in Recife, Brazil, on Thursday July 30, 2009, after the death of her husband, Arturo Gatti, was ruled a suicide. *Associated Press*

Assim que eu puder emocionalmente
irei falar com a imprensa.
Esta sendo uma dor inexplicavel
e insuportável essa perca e essa
maliciosa acusação.
Perdi meu marido!
A pessoa mais importante da minha vida.
Quem mes conhecia sabia o Tamanho
do nosso amor.
Sou inocente e sei que isso sera
provado em poucos dias.
Agradeço a todos meus familiares,
amigos e desconhecidos que Tem orado
e acreditado em mim.
A imprensa e a opinião do delegado
não me machuca. O que me fere
é saber do sofrimento dos meus
familiares e amigos. O que me
fere é saber que meu esposo
Não estará na minha casa esperando
a minha chegada.

Pai, Mãe, Irma e Filho
    Eu amo vocês!
Junior, ~~~~~ já já mamãe esta em casa!
                    Amanda Rodrigues

A photograph of the letter Amanda Rodrigues sent to the Associated
Press in Recife, Brazil on July 15, 2009. *Associated Press*

Arturo Gatti's mother, Ida, holds his WBC junior-welterweight world title belt as she leaves the church with his stepfather, Geraldo Di Francesco and family members after funeral services for her son in Montreal on July 20, 2009. *Associated Press*

Mourners gather after Gatti's funeral service.
Associated Press

Gatti with his then-fiancee, Erika Rivera, and their two-week-old daughter, Sofia Bella Gatti, in New York, April 12, 2006.
Associated Press

Micky Ward speaks on behalf of Arturo Gatti during Gatti's induction ceremony at the International Boxing Hall of Fame in Canastota, N.Y., Sunday, June 9, 2013. *Associated Press*

Ciolino's words; they are confident, forceful, mindful of an intended effect, mindful of his audience. That a forensic investigation should lead Ciolino to make character pronouncements is indicative of the role Gatti's character played in shaping people's understanding of what happened. Whether Gatti seemed capable of killing himself seems, in a sense, immaterial given the verdict of the investigation and the decade of silence on the matter since. Besides, Ciolino, at least in this bold pronouncement, was wrong. There were at least two occasions that disprove it—two people too, each who knew Arturo better than Ciolino ever could. However, that alone is not enough to invalidate Ciolino's findings. Leaving the investigation he conducted aside, what is interesting about Ciolino's words is that they reveal how confidently we can speak of people we know, and, by extension, our trust in the criteria we use in establishing that knowledge.

So who was Gatti in the minds of the people who knew him best? He was a warrior, of course, the word inked permanently into his stomach was as good a descriptor for Gatti as any other. He earned this reputation in the ring, where his capacity for enduring punishment had become, one fist at a time, mythological. He was a man who could endure absurd suffering. How easy, then, is it to assume this toughness extended beyond his body, that Gatti was psychically rugged too? The connection between physical toughness and what we might call "heart" is a natural one, such that no one of exceptional toughness is denied the psychical fortitude that complements it. No one could watch Gatti will himself to victory and doubt that he embodied this tangible and intangible toughness. Speaking to his cousin's grit, Lorenzo Gatti said it ran in the family: "Every Gatti has heart. We don't give up. We don't know how to give up."

It wasn't just that Gatti could take punishment though; it's that he triumphed in the face of it. Like the glacier breaking the surface, his toughness was but the exposed portion of a greater presence. Gatti wasn't a mere punch-sponge, he was a champion—he overcame. How, then, to reconcile a career of awe-inspiring toughness, of heart, of will, of triumph, with suicide? Suicide, in the context of Gatti's life appears a willed defeat—a defeat he could never recover from.

When a family loses one of its own to suicide, a panic descends. This panic is rooted in the need to understand, to quarantine this act of destruction, to make it intelligible before the suffering borne of mystery spreads. This process can be quick: if the family recognized the person as capable of suicide, a clear chain of causality, of logic, can be established between the episodes of a traumatic life and its cessation. And identifying this chain brings solace. At that point of death, the dead no longer suffer. And just as important, the living don't suffer for them. There is no more bearing witness, no more helplessness, no more hope, no more living tied to the mast in the tempest of another's turmoil. Yes, a suicide like Gatti's can rend a family's chronology, forcing parents to live the nightmare of burying their child, but it is beautiful in its power to liberate. It can be heroic.

But for a tough family, a fighting family, one that prides itself on never giving up—how might such a family reconcile its identity, reconcile its most famous, celebrated instantiation of that identity with suicide? Perhaps it can't.

In *Suicide and the Soul*, psychologist James Hillman suggests that "the decision about suicide does not belong to you alone" because so much of what is fundamental to you, what Hillman would call the soul, participates in the world. In removing ourselves from the world, we are making what seems like a personal decision. But that decision is personal only in its execution; the judgment it makes is not only about the individual but about the world he or she chooses to leave. Is there something in that judgment that explains why Fabricio categorically denies his brother's suicide? Bob McKown pressed Fabricio during an interview for the *48 Hours* documentary about Gatti's death. Throughout the interview, McKown gives Fabricio opportunities to concede the possibility of suicide. Fabricio will have none of it. "I believe my brother got murdered. And you know what? Nobody's gonna change my mind." Perhaps the impossibility of Gatti's death, the shock and denial that come at learning the nightmarish news, are at work here. Do those feelings get sublimated into something tenable—into a rejection not of death but its explanation? A rejection that preserves the values the suicide seemed to undermine? "My brother wasn't a coward like that, like other people are," explains Fabricio. "When somebody commits suicide, you know what, they're cowards. They cannot face their problems. My brother, like the type of person he was, he faced any problems." The possibility that Gatti was facing his problems that lonely night in Brazil, and decided on what he believed to be the best solution to them, is something Fabricio cannot credit. Perhaps there is too much at stake. Religion may figure in here too. A death left inexplicable in its inability to fit into the family metaphor becomes condemnable when viewed through a religious lens. And that condemnation only makes the possibility for suicide less likely, not because of anything that happened in life—but because of what awaits after it.

Nor is the testimony of coroners and toxicologists likely to convince a family of fighters. Medical investigations tell us about a body, and perhaps, in the condition of that body, a bit of what motivates a person to end his life. But the refrain among both Gatti's friends and family was that he couldn't have killed himself, and so what could an autopsy tell them to convince them otherwise? He had a cause of death, but it was hardly greater than his reason for living. "I never believed that he did that, that he took his own life—never," said Ward. "He had a son that he loved to death. He had a daughter, Sofia, that he loved to death. Two kids. He wouldn't do it. No way. I don't see it."

We should ask, though, whether it is reasonable to limit a person's capabilities to actions in keeping with our understanding of them. (Gatti's own career is instructive here: before he turned the impossible into a routine, he had first to surprise us.) We can never get so close to someone as to predict their behavior perfectly, refracted as others are through the lenses that color our picture of the world. Perhaps there is no way to breach the abyss between those trying to understand and those who can't be understood.

And so a sort of paradox exists, where the world confirms conflicting views. For those who knew him best, Gatti could not have killed himself. The evidence justifies this interpretation, and where it falters, where doubt cracks the foundation, belief buttresses it. Lynch describes this position perfectly, achingly: "There's so many conflicting stories. No one really knows the truth of what happened. But I believe, in my heart, no one knew him better than me in his adult life. I can guarantee you Arturo Gatti didn't take his life that night in Brazil. He was killed. He was murdered."

▼ ▼ ▼

By December 2011, the fighting was finally over. Quebec Superior Court Justice Claudine Roy sided against Ida and Fabricio Gatti in the civil trial they brought against Amanda, awarding Gatti's estimated $3.4 million fortune to his widow. The Gatti's had argued that an older will, one that preceded the one that Gatti drafted before his fateful trip to Brazil, should have been considered valid. That will left Gatti's estate to his mother and his daughter (though Fabricio said he would be willing to set up Junior with the same financial support as Sofia). The Gatti's could not produce a copy of the early will, however. So Justice Roy ruled Gatti's 2009 will was valid, and that he signed it without being manipulated into doing so by his wife. Amanda was thrilled at the ruling, one that not only afforded her the money she believed herself legally entitled to but also—in her eyes, at least—proved she did not control or manipulate her ex-husband into naming her the sole beneficiary of his estate.

The proceedings had been bitter. Amanda broke down while answering questions about her behavior before and after her husband's death, and about why she denied her in-laws access to her son. She admitted how difficult visitation would have been, knowing that Ida believed Amanda was a murderer. "I know I was not a perfect wife. I could have been better, I did a lot of bad things," she cried.

Some of the things Amanda admitted to were suspicious. Rather than use the notary a few blocks from their Montreal home, the same notary Arturo and Amanda had used repeatedly, she selected a new one (Moidel) from the phone book because she "wanted her own." While Amanda testified that her husband had accompanied her on every visit to the notary, Moidel said that the first time he met Amanda she was alone. Just days before Gatti was found dead, Amanda contacted the couple's financial advisor in New Jersey requesting he wire $300,000 to a joint bank account. The reason? Because the Gattis intended to be in Brazil for a few months. Then there was the $500,000 condominium in Montreal's Little Italy neighborhood that Gatti made an offer on. Amanda said she was supposed to move into it, but Gatti's friends testified the boxer purchased the condo for him and his son alone. The same day Gatti placed an offer on that condominium, a New Jersey lawyer contacted Amanda to tell her Gatti was pursuing a divorce. Still, Amanda didn't expect to be abandoned by her in-laws. Ida Gatti was unmoved, telling the court that Amanda was "not a good wife or mother," and that she was the reason Gatti took to drinking.

Fabricio had his behavior picked apart throughout the trial too. He said he searched exhaustively for a copy of his brother's previous will, even traveling to Gatti's New Jersey home. Fabricio denied checking Gatti's Montreal condo for the document, though, an omission that left Justice Roy incredulous. She was critical, too, of information Fabricio withheld. It was revealed that some of Gatti's personal effects, including tax returns, bills, and other documents, were being stored in Ida's basement. Fabricio knew about these items but did not tell his lawyer about them. More suspiciously, he admitted to angrily destroying some of his brother's mail in the months after Arturo died. As it turns out, Amanda wasn't quite hiding Junior from his family either. Fabricio testified that he'd made no real effort to see his nephew, assuming that Amanda would deny him the visit. But during the trial, Amanda told Ida that she was welcome to visit her grandson whenever she liked. Fabricio leaped at the opportunity, telling the court, "It was fun, we missed Junior a lot, he has his father's eyes." Tears welled in Amanda's.

What is so striking about the civil trial isn't the suspicion it casts about Amanda or Fabricio, however. What is so striking is the sadness. A grieving family, a grieving widow, locked in a fight over money both would happily forfeit to bring back the benefactor. Of course, the Gattis didn't believe that about Amanda. She had gotten what she always wanted, what she'd conspired and killed for. And Amanda, who had refused a settlement in the case even if further litigation threatened to exhaust her husband's fortune? She got what she believed she was legally entitled to. But did she get what she wanted? She walked free because, as Alberes said when the pressure to reopen the Gatti investigation mounted: that while Gatti's family may have been sickened by Amanda acquiring a fortune, there was no way to "imprison an innocent person." But is Amanda innocent? Can she ever be?

▼▼▼

The answer to that question isn't something Amanda concerns herself with today. Ten years later she has done her best to put the ordeal behind her. She works at a luxury vehicle dealership. She goes to church. She spends time with her son. She does all of this in Montreal, the city she says she fell in love with; the city many of her accusers still call home. She hasn't spoken to the Gattis since the civil trial ended.

Except for Joe.

He had his suspicions about Amanda, too. But Amanda reached out to him after being released from jail. She wanted him to visit her, wanted to set the record straight, he said. He acquiesced, using the visit as an opportunity to ascertain some proof of Amanda's dishonesty. He didn't find it. "What changed my mind is when I got to her house. . . . She showed up and I'm looking at her—there were no signs of anything. She looked at my eyes and it was nothing." Amanda put trust in Joe, something he admits helped her earn his own. When she traveled to Montreal in 2009, Amanda left Junior with his uncle. Joe remembers Junior's joy at seeing him. "He was just hugging me. He wouldn't let me go. I put him down, he wanted to play with me. . . . It was something else."

And what of the little boy? The one whose father would have given anything for, the one his mother says she owes her happiness, indeed her very life, to? He's ten years old now. He was only ten months old when his father died. But he knows his father, knows him from videos, from the trunks, posters, gloves, and championship belts that adorn his home. Perhaps he sees his father in the mirror. We are often a mix of our parents, our faces flashing this or that resemblance depending on the expression. Junior's smile is his father's; the way it makes his cheeks gently pinch his eyes is undeniable. How sweet that he can remind the world of his father with a smile. He knows what his name means; it's why the other kids regard him as they do, why Roy Jones Jr. and Mike Tyson have called him on the phone.

When he slips between the ropes in Ring 83 Boxing Club, where he has trained for two years, the resemblances continue. Moe Latif, who trains Junior, says the boy has the same footwork as his father, the same fighting passion, the same defensive lapses. Asked about his dreams, Junior says he wants to "become a five-time champion."

There may come a time when he too wonders what happened to his father in Brazil. Why an entire branch of his family tree has been pruned from his life, why so much money, time, and effort was put into denying his father's suicide. He'll read the stories, he'll hear people talk. It seems impossible that Junior will move through life without confronting the conflicting explanations for the glaring absence in it. The wiring for that confrontation was laid years ago. And it is live. When that moment comes, may he meet it with his father's resolve. A fighter's resolve.

SELECTED SOURCES

A number of sources were consulted for this book: Associated Press, badlefthook.com, boxingnewsonline.net, boxingscene.com, boxingmonthly.com, cbc.ca, cbsnews.com, citynews.ca, cnn.com, ctvnews.ca, deadspin.com, esquire.com, globalnews.ca, theglobeandmail.com, grantland.com, theguardian.com, hbo.com, irishcentral.com, irishtimes.com, www.nj.com/jjournal/, journaldemontreal.com/, latimes.com, newjersey.com, nydailynews.com, nypost.com, nytimes.com, ringtv.com, sportingnews.com, sportsnet.ca, tcpalm.com, thestar.com, tvasports.ca.

SPECIAL THANKS

To Kathy Duva, who agreed to be interviewed for this book, and to Nicole Duva and Matthew Swain for arranging the interview. Thank you to Jude Star, a psychotherapist in training in Toronto, for many insightful discussions about suicide. Thanks to Alan Conceição who proved incredibly helpful in the research process.

ABOUT THE AUTHOR

Jimmy Tobin is a member of the Boxing Writers Association of America. His work has appeared in Hannibal Boxing, The Cruelest Sport, 15 Rounds, Esquina Boxeo, El Malpensante, The Queensbury Rules, and The Fight Network. He teaches at George Brown College in Toronto.

Killed in Brazil? is set in 9.5-point Palatino, which was designed by Hermann Zapf and released initially in 1949 by the Stempel foundry and later by other companies, most notably the Mergenthaler Linotype Company. Named after the sixteenth-century Italian master of calligraphy Giovanni Battista Palatino, Palatino is based on the humanist typefaces of the Italian Renaissance, and reflects Zapf's expertise as a calligrapher. Copyeditor for this project was Shannon LeMay-Finn. The book was designed by Brad Norr Design, Minneapolis, Minnesota, and typeset by New Best-set Typesetters Ltd. Printed and manufactured by Short Run Press Ltd on acid-free paper.

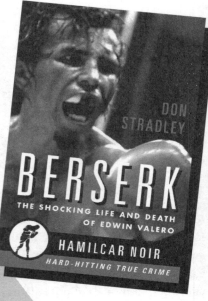

ALSO READ

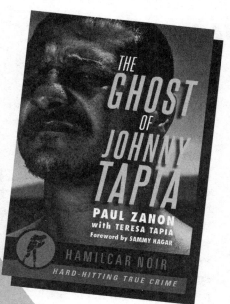

ALSO READ

HAMILCAR NOIR | TRUE CRIME LIBRARY #3

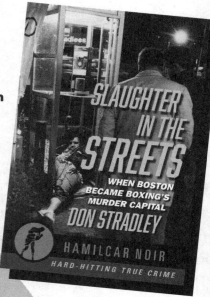

"A female stenographer who had been at her desk filling out Christmas cards looked on in horror; the sound of guns a moment earlier had shattered the holiday mood, and now she was confronted by the sight of Frankie in the doorway, blood gushing from his wounds. Without saying a word, he walked in and sat in a chair. Then he pitched forward, dead."

Boston was once a thriving boxing city. And it was also host to an ever-expanding underworld. From the early days of Boston's Mafia, to the era of Whitey Bulger, many of the city's boxers found themselves drawn to the criminal life. Most of them ended up dead. *Slaughter in the Streets*, by Don Stradley, tells the violent and often tragic story of these misguided young men who thought their toughness in the ring could protect them from the most cold-blooded killers in the country.

Find *Slaughter in the Streets* at your favorite bookstore or online retailer! Or order online at www.hamilcarpubs.com.

ISBN 9781949590258 | Paperback | February 2020

HAMILCAR NOIR

HARD-HITTING TRUE CRIME

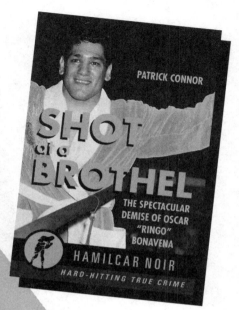

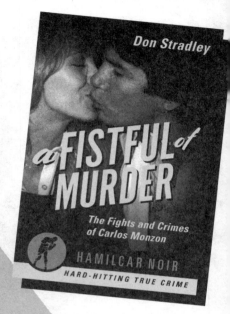